Bridge for Absolute Beginners

B. T. Batsford, *London*

First published 2001

ISBN 0 7134 8618 X

Typeset by Wakewing, High Wycombe
Printed by Redwood Books, Trowbridge, Wilts
for the publishers,
B. T. Batsford, 9 Blenheim Court, Brewery Road, London N7 9NT
A member of the Chrysalis Group plc

A BATSFORD BRIDGE BOOK
Series Editor: Phil King

Contents

Introduction

Robert Sheehan was the bridge correspondent of *The Times* from 1994 until the end of 1999. For most of that time Sally Brock was his assistant; then for the first half of 2000, before a successor to Sheehan was found, Sally wrote the column under her own name. For the whole of this six-year period, an effort was made to cater for less experienced players and Friday became 'beginners' day'. After a few years of struggling to find suitable material for the Friday articles, it was decided to start a complete course for beginners. The idea was that regular readers of *The Times* column could point their non-bridge-playing friends in the direction of these articles, or perhaps use them to help their non-bridge-playing friends to learn. The articles were remarkably popular. Unfortunately, the Sheehan/Brock stint at *The Times* came to an end before the course reached its natural conclusion and many readers were disappointed. This book is an attempt to remedy that disappointment. Here is a complete beginners' course, starting with the mechanics of the game, proceeding through MiniBridge, and the early stages of bidding and cardplay, leaving the reader at the end of the course with a sound basic grounding in bridge. There is a strong emphasis throughout the book on getting lots of practice. The lessons will be better understood if the reader keeps a pack of cards near and deals out the cards for himself.

Many people have contributed in some way to this book. Particular thanks must go to Pat Husband for her help, both with the original articles and in proof-reading the final book. Thanks also to David Mills for proof-reading and Jim Goodison whose articles in *Young Bridge* (the English Bridge Union's publication aimed at young people) formed the base for several of the articles on MiniBridge.

Part I
Mechanics and MiniBridge

Even complete bridge beginners have different degrees of knowledge about the game. We believe in making no assumptions and have written this course to cater for people who are unfamiliar with a pack of cards. So those of you who are used to cards, and especially trick-taking games, may wish to skip the first few lessons on the basics.

There are two components to the game of bridge: the bidding and the play. The bidding comes first but is difficult to understand until you have begun to master the play. MiniBridge, which is one of the best developments the teaching of bridge has seen in recent years, enables you to play through a bridge deal without getting bogged down in theoretical discussion about the bidding. Effectively, it is 'bridge without the bidding'. Only when you have become familiar with the play of the cards will we move on to bidding.

Lesson 1
Preliminaries

Bridge is a card game for four players, played with a standard pack of 52 playing cards which is divided into four suits:

spades (♠)	hearts (♡)
diamonds (♢)	clubs (♣)

Make certain the pack has no jokers. If you have led a sheltered life and this is unfamiliar to you, get a pack of cards in your hand and familiarise yourself with the suits.

You will see that each suit has thirteen cards. Nine of them are numbered in straightforward fashion, from two to ten. The other four cards are the *jack* (J), the *queen* (Q), the *king* (K) and the *ace* (A). These four cards are, in ascending order, the most important cards in the pack. The complete order is:

2 3 4 5 6 7 8 9 10 J Q K A

The players are in two *partnerships*, and the two *partners* sit opposite each other. You can play in prearranged partnerships, or you can select the partnerships by 'cutting for partners'. To do that, you spread the pack of cards on the table face down, and each player takes (or 'cuts') a card. The two players selecting the two highest cards play together against the other two players. That brings us to the first point about the use of the cards: their rank. In bridge (though not in every card game), aces are the highest cards, followed in descending order by king, queen, jack and ten (those five cards are called *honour* cards). Then the other cards rank in their normal numerical order.

We will consider later what happens when in the cutting for partners two players cut a card of the same *rank* (say the nine of diamonds and the nine of clubs). For the time being, if that happens those two players should just cut again.

The player cutting the highest card distributes or *deals* the cards. There is a ritual about the actual process of shuffling and dealing, but the basis is that the cards should be well mixed by the non-dealing partnership, and then distributed by the dealer. He starts by giving a card face down to the opponent on his left and then continues in a clockwise direction giving one card at a time to each player, until all 52 cards have been dealt. So how many cards does each player get? Fifty-two divided by four, which is thirteen. His thirteen cards are referred to as his *hand*.

Get a *pack* (or 'deck') of cards and select this hand from it

♠ AQ42
♡ AJ3
♢ 1032
♣ Q95

That is your first bridge hand.

Lesson 2
Displaying the hand

In the last lesson we asked you to get a pack of cards and select this hand from it:

♠ AQ42
♡ AJ3
♢ 1032
♣ Q95

It is easiest if you start with a pack already arranged into suits. You should have picked out the ace, queen, four and two of spades, the ace, jack and three of hearts, the ten, three and two of diamonds and the queen, nine and five of clubs.

Now pick up the hand and practise holding it so nobody else can see it. It is best to sort it into suits, with the highest card in the suit on your left. Although bridge hands are always written down in the sequence spades, hearts, diamonds, clubs (♠, ♡, ♢, ♣), it is convenient to arrange them in your hand by alternating red and black suits. That way you are less likely to suffer the ignominy of confusing the two of hearts with the two of diamonds (though that happens to players at all levels, we can assure you). Hold the cards in a fan, so that you just see the symbols at the top left-hand corner of the individual cards. It should look like this.

When we write individual hands in the text we do it in two ways, either down the page as above, or sometimes across the page like this:

♠ AQ42 ♡ AJ3 ♢ 1032 ♣ Q95

The four players' hands make up the deal. When we show a full deal, this is how it looks on paper:

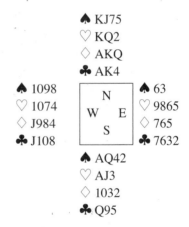

```
            ♠ KJ75
            ♡ KQ2
            ♢ AKQ
            ♣ AK4
♠ 1098                    ♠ 63
♡ 1074      N            ♡ 9865
♢ J984   W     E         ♢ 765
♣ J108      S            ♣ 7632
            ♠ AQ42
            ♡ AJ3
            ♢ 1032
            ♣ Q95
```

You will notice the square in the middle of the diagram has the letters NESW marked; they stand for the compass points North, East, South and West, and are useful for talking about the deal. North and South are partners, playing against East and West. Lay the deal out with your pack of cards.

Lesson 3
The trick

After the cards have been dealt, there are two phases of the game: first the *auction* and then the *play*. In this series of lessons, we are going to concentrate in some detail on the play, before considering the auction. For the time being, all you need to know about the auction is that it determines the *final contract*, and who is *declarer*. These terms will be explained later.

The unit of the play in bridge is the *trick*: the play proceeds trick by trick. A trick is a collection of four cards, one from each player. So how many tricks are there in a deal? Thirteen, because each player is dealt thirteen cards, and contributes one to each trick. These are the rules of the trick: the first person to contribute a card to a trick is said to be 'on lead', and he can choose to play any card in his hand face up on the table. Then the remaining players play to the trick in clockwise order. If they have cards in the suit led, they must play one of them – referred to as *following suit*. The trick is won by the person playing the highest card to the trick. As an example, let us say West (remember the compass points used for describing the position of the players round the table) is on lead, and he decides to lead the two of hearts. This might be the structure of the trick:

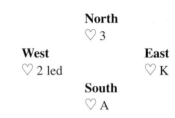

Order of play: West, North, East, South.

Each player followed with hearts, as they all had cards in the suit; North played the three, East the king, and South the ace. Who won the trick?

If you remember from Lesson 1, we said the rank of the cards within a particular suit is that the ace is the highest, followed by the king, queen, jack; then the remainder of the suit has its normal numerical order. So here the highest card played on the trick is the ace of hearts, and South wins the trick. The winner of the trick has to lead to the next one, so in this case South will lead to the next trick.

The aim of each partnership is to win as many tricks as possible, and for this purpose it doesn't matter which of the partners wins the trick. In this case the opening leader (West) and second player (North) played small cards and the third and last players (East and South) high cards – quite a common structure for a trick.

Lesson 4
Tricks: trumping and discarding

In the last lesson we started discussing the *trick*, the unit by which the play phase of bridge proceeds. The winner of the trick leads to the next trick. Say in the example below South had won the previous trick and now decides to lead the queen of diamonds.

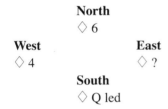

Play proceeds clockwise. West plays the four of diamonds and North the six.

East is still to play, and he has no diamonds. If he had a diamond, he would have to play it (failing to do so would be *revoking*, which incurs blood-curdling penalties); but if he has no diamond he can play what he likes. If the contract is a *suit* contract, one of the four suits will be *trumps*. That suit has a status higher than the other three suits – any card in it will beat any card in the other three suits (referred to as the *plain suits*). In the example above, if clubs were trumps and East had no diamonds he could play the two of clubs on the queen of diamonds, and would win the trick. That is known as *trumping* or *ruffing*.

But sometimes there are no trumps (*no-trumps*). In that case, no suit has a preferential rank; the only way East could win this trick would be to play a diamond higher than the queen (i.e. the ace or king), and as we have assumed he has no diamonds, he cannot do that. He must play a card of some other suit (known as *discarding*), and South wins the trick.

There are two methods of keeping track of how many tricks have been won by each side. The more common way in casual games is for one of the partners to gather together the cards of a trick his side has won and stack them face down in front of him. He should keep each trick separate, so that the other players at the table can see how many tricks his side has won.

The other method, which is used in tournaments and which we recommend for those learning the game, is for each player to keep his own cards in front of him, stacking them face down starting on his left. If he loses the trick he puts the card with the long axis parallel to the table, and if he wins the trick he puts the long axis perpendicular to the table.

The advantage of this method is that you can later reconstruct how the play went.

Lesson 5
The dummy

In most trick-taking games, e.g. whist, each player plays his own hand. But in bridge one of the players is called the *declarer*. (That is something determined in the auction phase of the game.) The other side are the *defenders*. When the play starts the declarer's partner puts his whole hand face up on the table. It is called the *dummy*. Dummy takes no part in the play – the declarer is in charge of both hands. Although the declarer can be any of the players at the table, the usual convention when writing about the game is to have South (or occasionally West, for reasons of space) as declarer. Hence North is dummy.

In bridge literature, the dummy is always written like this:

♠ KJ75
♡ KQ2
♢ AK10
♣ AK4

But when actually playing the game dummy puts his hand down with the suits in columns, like this:

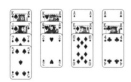

There is no preferred sequence, except that if it is a trump contract the trump suit should be on the left from declarer's viewpoint (i.e. if the above hand were played in a suit contract spades would be trumps).

To give an example of declarer's responsibilities:

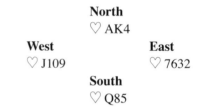

North
♡ AK4
West　　　　　　**East**
♡ J109　　　　　　♡ 7632
South
♡ Q85

West leads the jack of hearts, and then declarer decides what card to play from dummy. Provided he plays the ace, king, and queen separately on each trick, he can make three tricks. But he has to be careful not to play, for example, the ace from dummy and the queen from his hand – that would eventually cost a trick. Lay it out and practise taking all three tricks with the North-South cards.

One final thought about these bridge lessons (and bridge articles in general). No matter how well bridge is taught, the material will not jump off the page and rewire your brain without some effort from you. If you expect to browse through it with the attention you would give a gossip column, you won't learn much. You must put the concentration into it that you would do for say a crossword, or a chess problem.

Lesson 6
MiniBridge 1

As we said in a previous lesson, bridge is composed of two phases: the *bidding* followed by the *play*. In the 'Time before MiniBridge' bridge teachers had to struggle with the Catch-22 problem that the bidding is incomprehensible to anyone who doesn't understand the rudiments of the play, but the play cannot commence until the bidding is over.

MiniBridge was invented (in Holland and France virtually simultaneously but with slightly different rules) to circumvent this difficulty. It is a way to start playing bridge without bothering with the bidding. When everyone is familiar with the procedures of play, then the bidding can be added.

The preliminaries are as we have described earlier. Four players sit down and perhaps cut for partners. The shuffle and deal take place just as for bridge. Everyone picks up their cards and sorts them. The next thing is for each player to add up his *high-card points*. Generally speaking, high-ranking cards are more likely to take tricks than low-ranking ones, honour cards taking more tricks than non-honour cards. Aces take more tricks than kings, which take more tricks than queens, etc. The point-count system (which you will also meet when you move on to bridge proper) is a system designed to compare the strengths of different hands. In the point-count system:

an ace (A)	=	4 points
a king (K)	=	3 points
a queen (Q)	=	2 points
a jack (J)	=	1 point

There are ten points in each suit, 40 in the whole pack. Using your ever-present pack of cards, sorted into the four suits, make up the following two hands and count how many high-card points they hold:

♠ AK64	♠ Q10873
♡ QJ82	♡ AK7
♢ Q42	♢ AJ3
♣ KJ	♣ Q7

Of course, both are worth 16 points.

The dealer starts by announcing how many points he holds. Then, in a clockwise direction, the other players do likewise. Remember, it should add up to 40. If it doesn't, have a recount. Then the two partners, those sitting opposite each other, North and South or East and West, add their point-count totals together. The side with the higher total becomes the *declaring side*; the other side, their opponents, become the *defending side*. (If each partnership has 20, redeal and start again.) And the member of that partnership with the higher number (or the first to speak if they have the same) becomes declarer.

Lesson 7
MiniBridge 2

So, it's time to look at our first example. Make sure you have a pack of cards (sorted into four suits) and make up the following four hands as North, East, South and West:

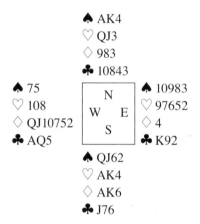

♠ AK4
♡ QJ3
♢ 983
♣ 10843

♠ 75   ♠ 10983
♡ 108   ♡ 97652
♢ QJ10752   ♢ 4
♣ AQ5   ♣ K92

♠ QJ62
♡ AK4
♢ AK6
♣ J76

South (the dealer) starts by announcing that he has 18 points. West has 9, North 10 and East 3. North-South have 28 (18+10) and East-West 12 (9+3), so North-South are the declaring side. South has more than North so he becomes declarer.

At this point dummy is put down, i.e. North puts his cards face up on the table. These should be arranged tidily, one card half behind another, in four columns, one for each suit, as we illustrated in Lesson 5.

Declarer now considers the two hands together and decides if he wants to select a suit to be trumps or if he should play in no-trumps. In general, and certainly to start with, you should count the number of cards in your combined longest suit. Here you have seven spades, six hearts, six diamonds and seven clubs. If your longest suit is eight cards or more, you should choose that as trumps (with two suits the same length choose the one containing the most points), otherwise choose no-trumps. So, South announces that he will play in no-trumps.

It is now up to West, the hand on declarer's left, to make the *opening lead*, i.e. to play the first card to the first trick. When defending against no-trumps it usually works best to lead your longest suit. And if you have an *honour sequence* (i.e. three or more consecutive honour cards) in that suit you should lead the top of it. Here West should lead the queen of diamonds.

South's aim is to win as many tricks as possible. On this deal he should make four tricks in spades, three tricks in hearts and two in diamonds. Note that he can make four tricks in spades because he has four cards in the suit and he has the ace, king, queen and jack. Provided he plays only one of those honours to each trick he will make four tricks. However, in hearts he has only three-card suits and, although he also has the ace, king, queen and jack, he can only ever make three tricks because at some time two of his honours will fall on the same trick.

Before reading on, play out the hand and see how many tricks you can make.

Lesson 8
MiniBridge 3

This is the hand we were looking at in the previous lesson:

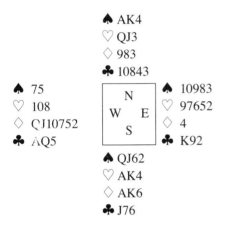

```
              ♠ AK4
              ♡ QJ3
              ◇ 983
              ♣ 10843
♠ 75                         ♠ 10983
♡ 108         N              ♡ 97652
◇ QJ10752   W   E            ◇ 4
♣ AQ5         S              ♣ K92
              ♠ QJ62
              ♡ AK4
              ◇ AK6
              ♣ J76
```

In the last lesson we left you trying to make as many tricks as possible as South in no-trumps.

There are various successful ways to play this hand. One way would be to win the first trick with the king of diamonds, and then play the two of spades to dummy's ace. Now lead the king of spades and play the six of spades from hand. The next trick should be dummy's four of spades played to the queen in your hand. Now play the jack of spades, discarding a club or a diamond from the dummy. You have taken your four spade tricks. Now move on to hearts. Play the ace from your hand and the three from dummy. Then the king from your hand and the jack from dummy. Finally play the four from

your hand and the queen from dummy. The last trick you have to take is the ace of diamonds in your hand. You have made nine tricks.

Of course, South is not the only person playing this game. South is trying to make as many tricks as possible and East-West are trying to stop him doing so and make as many as they can themselves. On this hand there was not much for them to do as South took the first nine tricks and then more or less gave up, but it is not always like that. It is important to watch like a hawk when you are on the defending side because you and your partner are trying to frustrate the declarer and must try to work together. Concentrate and think about what declarer is trying to do and what your partner is trying to achieve with you. Remember that on average you defend twice as many hands as you declare; you will miss much of the interest that MiniBridge (or bridge) has to offer if you do not take defence seriously. Many of the best players find defence the most exciting and fun part of the game because a successful partnership understanding is extremely satisfying. And the times when you are dummy give you the best opportunity of observing when the other three players are doing the right thing and where they are going wrong.

Lesson 9
MiniBridge 4

Although we shall give several instructive MiniBridge deals in this book, it will take you a very long time to learn if they are the only hands you play. It is of vital importance to play as often as you can. Practise, practise, practise.

Here is another example. Once more, much the easiest way to follow the play is to deal out the hands for yourself.

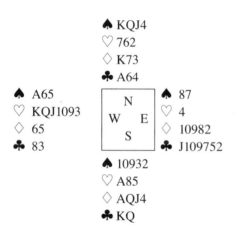

```
                ♠ KQJ4
                ♡ 762
                ◇ K73
                ♣ A64
♠ A65        ┌─────────┐   ♠ 87
♡ KQJ1093    │    N    │   ♡ 4
◇ 65         │  W   E  │   ◇ 10982
♣ 83         │    S    │   ♣ J109752
             └─────────┘
                ♠ 10932
                ♡ A85
                ◇ AQJ4
                ♣ KQ
```

Again (for convenience) South is dealer and announces his 16 points. West has 10, North 13 and East just 1. South is declarer and North puts his dummy down.

Suppose for the moment that South chooses to play in no-trumps. West has great hopes of taking a lot of tricks against a no-trump contract. He leads his king of hearts which declarer wins with the ace. Declarer now plays the king of clubs from his hand which wins the trick and then the queen of clubs which also wins the trick. He then plays the four of diamonds to dummy's king. Declarer plays the ace of clubs from dummy discarding a heart from hand.

West needs to pay attention now. He has no clubs left so has to discard. He must be careful not to discard a heart which may be a winner later. He discards the five of spades. Declarer now plays the three of diamonds from dummy and the ace from his hand. Now the queen of diamonds from hand and again West must discard – the six of spades this time. Declarer now plays the jack of diamonds from his hand and this time West does have to discard a heart.

But declarer has taken all the tricks he can: one heart, four diamonds and three in clubs, eight in all. When he plays a spade, West wins his ace and takes four heart tricks.

Note that declarer had to be careful to take all his tricks. Suppose he wins the heart lead and first takes his diamond tricks. He is in his own hand after taking the last winner and can now cash the king and queen of clubs but he has no way of reaching dummy's ace. He would have to play a spade but West would win and cash all his heart winners. One of declarer's winners has disappeared.

Lesson 10
MiniBridge 5

This is the hand we looked at in Lesson 9:

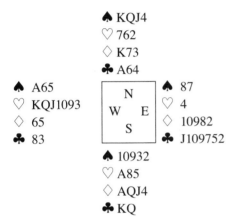

```
              ♠ KQJ4
              ♡ 762
              ◇ K73
              ♣ A64
♠ A65         ┌─────────┐    ♠ 87
♡ KQJ1093     │    N    │    ♡ 4
◇ 65          │  W   E  │    ◇ 10982
♣ 83          │    S    │    ♣ J109752
              └─────────┘
              ♠ 10932
              ♡ A85
              ◇ AQJ4
              ♣ KQ
```

South, with his 16 points, became declarer and North put his dummy down.

Previously we supposed that South chose to play in no-trumps. West led the king of hearts. Both declarer and West played well thereafter and declarer came to eight tricks (one heart, four diamonds and three clubs).

This hand is a good example of why it is usually right to choose a trump suit when there are eight cards or more of a suit between the two hands. Here, if you count the cards in the different suits in the North and South hands added together, you find that they have eight spades, six hearts, seven diamonds and five clubs. Suppose that instead of choosing to play in no-trumps, South had chosen his best *fit*, spades, as trumps. No doubt West would still choose to

lead the king of hearts and South would win his ace.

One of the problems of playing with a trump suit is working out whether or not to play trumps straight away and we will address that problem in a later article. But here let us asume declarer plays trumps immediately. At trick two he plays a trump. West wins his ace and plays the queen of hearts followed by the jack of hearts, but he can't take as many heart tricks as he did against the no-trump contract. If he plays the ten of hearts declarer will play a trump from one hand or the other – let us say he chooses to trump in dummy with the king. Then he plays the queen of spades followed by the jack of spades which draws everyone's trumps. Now he will make the rest of the tricks, ten in all. Two tricks more than he made in no-trumps.

Lesson 11
MiniBridge 6

You should now have played through two hands in MiniBridge and should be beginning to understand some of the concepts of trick-taking. Until now declarer has simply been aiming to 'take as many tricks as possible'. This is fine but after you have been playing for a while you will find it more interesting to set yourself targets. Although some hands fit together better than others, the following is a rough guide as to how many tricks you should try to take with different combined point counts:

Points	Number of tricks
21–22	7
23–24	8
25–26	9
27–28	10
29–32	11
33–36	12
37+	13

Let's look at some examples. This time West is declarer:

♠ AK3   N   ♠ QJ542
♡ A762   W   E   ♡ K83
♢ KQ2   S   ♢ A53
♣ K43   ♣ A9

Here East-West have 33 combined points (West has 19 and East 14). West should aim to make twelve tricks. It looks as if he will

succeed this time as he will make five spades, two hearts, three diamonds and two clubs, whether he chooses to play in spades or no-trumps.

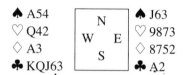

♠ A54   N   ♠ J63
♡ Q42   W   E   ♡ 9873
♢ A3   S   ♢ 8752
♣ KQJ63   ♣ A2

Here East-West have 21 combined points (West has 16 and East 5). West should aim to make seven tricks in no-trumps, which again looks just what he will do with five clubs, one spade and one diamond.

Take out your pack of cards, set out the above hands and play them through to make sure you make the right number of tricks. Make sure that you always lead from the hand that took the last trick.

We have deliberately chosen very straightforward hands to illustrate the point. In real life it is not so simple. Some hands 'fit' well together while others do not. Change the second example above so that East has the ace of hearts instead of the ace of clubs. Now, with exactly the same number of points, it is difficult to be sure of more than five tricks. Nevertheless, setting targets makes the game more interesting. In a later lesson, we will cover this subject in more depth and we will start to use targets that are of more relevance to bridge proper.

Lesson 12
MiniBridge 7

So far every example hand we have seen has been concerned with 'top tricks', i.e. you just needed to cash your aces, king and queens. In real life this is not what usually happens. Instead, you need to *establish* tricks. This means that you need to force out a high card from an opponent, in order to establish a lower honour card in your own hand. For example, suppose you hold KQ5 of a suit in your hand and 432 in the dummy. There are no tricks to cash in this suit because you do not have the ace. But if you play the king, an opponent will win his ace and your queen will be established as a winner.

Here is an example hand:

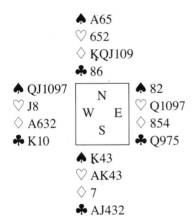

```
              ♠ A65
              ♡ 652
              ◇ KQJ109
              ♣ 86
  ♠ QJ1097   ┌─────┐   ♠ 82
  ♡ J8       │  N  │   ♡ Q1097
  ◇ A632     │W   E│   ◇ 854
  ♣ K10      │  S  │   ♣ Q975
             └─────┘
              ♠ K43
              ♡ AK43
              ◇ 7
              ♣ AJ432
```

South is the dealer and the players announce their points as follows: South 15, West 11, North 10, East 4. So, South becomes declarer and North puts down dummy. With 25 points between the two hands the target is nine tricks. With no more than a seven-card fit in any suit, South chooses to play no-trumps.

Before reading further, make up these hands and prepare to play through the deal as you read.

West leads his longest suit, spades, and as it is headed by a sequence (three or more consecutive cards) he leads the top of it, i.e. the queen. South has only five 'top tricks' (two spades, two hearts and one club) but his target is nine tricks so he must first establish four more by playing a diamond. When a defender wins his ace, there will be four established diamond tricks in the dummy.

So, South wins the king of spades in his hand and plays a diamond. West wins the ace and plays another spade. South wins the trick with dummy's ace and plays the queen of diamonds, followed by the jack of diamonds, followed by the ten and nine of diamonds. He discards small cards from his hand and then cashes the ace and king of hearts and ace of clubs to make nine tricks in all.

To learn more from this useful hand, try taking the first trick in dummy with the ace of spades. See what happens when declarer tries to establish the diamond suit. He plays the king of diamonds and West wins his ace and plays another spade as before. There are four diamond winners in the dummy but there is no way to reach them, i.e. dummy has no *entry*.

Lesson 13
MiniBridge 8

It is not always easy to decide whether you want to play a hand in a suit contract or in no-trumps. Until now you have been given a simple rule that when you have eight cards in a suit you choose that suit as trumps, otherwise you play in no-trumps. This is a useful guideline but it doesn't mean you can't use your brain to depart from the rule.

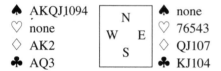

♠ AKQJ1094   ♠ none
♡ none   ♡ 76543
♢ AK2   ♢ QJ107
♣ AQ3   ♣ KJ104

Here East-West do not have more than a seven-card fit in any suit, but there are eight top hearts missing so in no-trumps North-South are likely to cash five or six tricks in this suit before declarer can stop them. In spades, on the other hand, declarer will trump (or *ruff*) the opening lead, draw all the trumps and make all thirteen tricks.

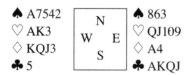

♠ A7542   ♠ 863
♡ AK3   ♡ QJ109
♢ KQJ3   ♢ A4
♣ 5   ♣ AKQJ

This time East-West have thirteen tricks in no-trumps (one spade, four hearts, four diamonds and four clubs), but their best fit, spades, is fraught with danger. If the opposing five cards *divide* (or *break*) 3-2, West will make eleven

tricks, but if spades break 4-1 or 5-0, he will have to settle for ten or even nine.

Get out your pack and play through the two pairs of hands given above; make sure you agree with me about the consequences of playing with spades as trumps.

The most common reason for choosing a no-trump contract when there is an eight-card trump fit is that the quality of the trump suit is poor and there is plenty of strength outside. The most common reason for choosing a trump suit when there is no eight-card fit is that there is a good long suit but one of the other suits is wide open.

In the last lesson we started to look at the *management of entries*. Entry problems are often easier in a suit contract because low cards can be ruffed, so trumps, in addition to high cards, can be used as entries.

♠ none   ♠ AKQJ109
♡ A5432   ♡ 6
♢ A876   ♢ J32
♣ A876   ♣ 432

Here, if West chooses no-trumps because he has no eight-card fit, he may not make many more than his three aces. However, with spades as trumps, it is much better. Make up and play out the hand. You should make at least nine tricks, thus confirming the superiority of the trump contract.

Lesson 14
MiniBridge 9

Obviously, it is possible to play a suit contract just like no-trumps, i.e. draw trumps and cash or establish winners, but the presence of a trump suit adds another dimension, that of *ruffing* (or *trumping*). Here is an example:

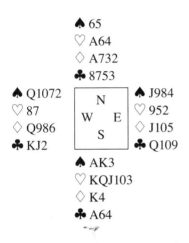

```
              ♠ 65
              ♡ A64
              ◇ A732
              ♣ 8753
♠ Q1072    ┌─────────┐   ♠ J984
♡ 87       │    N    │   ♡ 952
◇ Q986     │  W   E  │   ◇ J105
♣ KJ2      │    S    │   ♣ Q109
           └─────────┘
              ♠ AK3
              ♡ KQJ103
              ◇ K4
              ♣ A64
```

South is the dealer and the points are announced: South 20, West 8, North 8 and East 4. South becomes declarer. North puts down the dummy. With a combined 28 points, what should be the target?

Make up the hand and play in no-trumps. There are ten tricks (your normal target with 28 points) *on top* (two spades, five hearts, two diamonds and one club). But for those of you who like to exceed targets, consider playing with hearts as trumps. There are eight trumps of good quality, so it is unlikely that hearts will play any worse than no-trumps.

Before reading further, play out the hand with hearts as trumps and the opening lead of the two of spades. See if you can make an extra trick.

This time West did not have a clear choice of opening lead, with no convenient sequence of honours. We would choose the two of spades. We generally prefer to lead away from a queen rather than a king – declarer too often has the ace and the queen and makes an extra trick. We choose the two because it is normal to lead the lowest from a three- or four-card suit (more about that later).

You, South, win the spade lead with the ace when East plays the jack, and lay down the king and queen of hearts. In a trump contract you should always draw as many trumps as you can afford just in case your opponents make extra tricks by ruffing instead of you. Here you have only one spade to ruff so you need to leave only one trump in the dummy. Because your trumps in hand are so strong, you can afford to ruff with dummy's ace, just in case East also has a doubleton spade and could overruff dummy's six. After the king and queen of hearts, cash the king of spades and ruff a spade with dummy's ace. Now play a diamond to your king and draw the remaining trumps. When you have cashed your other top winners you will find that you have eleven winners, one more than you had in no-trumps.

Lesson 15
MiniBridge 10

It is important to understand the power of a good *fit*. The high-card points that you count at the start of every deal (and you will also do this when you move on to bridge proper) are only a guide to trick-taking potential; the guide works well when the combined hands are fairly balanced, i.e. when no really long suits are held. But long suits in a hand that fits well with partner's can make many more tricks than the point count would suggest.

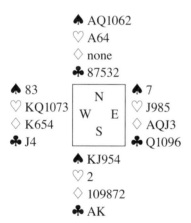

```
               ♠ AQ1062
               ♡ A64
               ◇ none
               ♣ 87532
  ♠ 83         ┌─────────┐   ♠ 7
  ♡ KQ1073     │    N    │   ♡ J985
  ◇ K654       │ W     E │   ◇ AQJ3
  ♣ J4         │    S    │   ♣ Q1096
               └─────────┘
               ♠ KJ954
               ♡ 2
               ◇ 109872
               ♣ AK
```

West is the dealer and the points are announced: West 9, North 10, East 10 and South 11. South is declarer. North puts down the dummy. With a combined 21 points, the target should be seven tricks. Make up the hand and play it in no-trumps with the lead of the king of hearts.

You probably made the eight tricks that were there on top (five spades, one heart and

two clubs). South's diamonds are strong enough to prevent East-West taking more than four tricks in the suit, however their cards are distributed.

Now play the hand with spades as trumps after the same opening lead. Look what happens. South wins with the ace in dummy, draws trumps in two rounds, cashes the ace and king of clubs and takes ruffs in one hand and then the other. There are endless variations but one would be: win the ace of hearts, cash the ace and king of spades, cash the ace and king of clubs, ruff a diamond, ruff a heart, ruff a diamond, ruff a heart, ruff a diamond with dummy's last trump, ruff a club with your last trump. That makes eleven tricks in all.

That sounds good, doesn't it? But you could have done even better. Don't draw trumps at all. Win the ace of hearts and ruff a heart, cash the ace and king of clubs, ruff a diamond and ruff a heart. Now all you have left are the AQ10 of spades and three clubs in dummy and the KJ9 of spades and three diamonds in hand. Your trumps are high so all you need to do is alternately ruff diamonds and clubs until you have made all the tricks. You have made all thirteen tricks for which you are supposed to need 37 combined points and you had only 21. This is known as *cross-ruffing*.

Take the time to play out the alternatives suggested because this helps you to see how to conjure up extra tricks.

Lesson 16
MiniBridge 11

On average you defend twice as many hands as you declare. Many players find defence harder than declarer play, though it can be the most exciting and fun part of the game.

So far there has been little instruction on defence and we now aim to remedy that by starting where the defence has to start, with the opening lead. You will learn some differences in defence against no-trumps and a contract with a trump suit, but we will start with no-trumps.

We have suggested previously that the top card of a sequence is a good lead. It is, but when you are defending against no-trumps you aim to establish tricks for the long cards in a suit, expecting your honour cards to make tricks in any event.

♠ A72
♥ QJ10
♦ J9873
♣ A6

Suppose that you are West defending against no-trumps. The safe lead is the queen of hearts. To lead the top card of a sequence (i.e. a 'run' of three or more cards) is a *convention* that most people follow. A convention is a rule that you and your partner have agreed on to enable you to learn something about each other's holding (or hand). In defence you must help partner as much as you can. When you lead the top card, partner knows that you

have the card immediately below it and don't have the card above it.

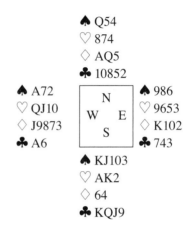

♠ Q54
♥ 874
♦ AQ5
♣ 10852

♠ A72 ♠ 986
♥ QJ10 ♥ 9653
♦ J9873 ♦ K102
♣ A6 ♣ 743

♠ KJ103
♥ AK2
♦ 64
♣ KQJ9

Your lead of the queen of hearts will knock out declarer's king. His goal with 25 points is nine tricks. He will attack spades. You will win with the ace and continue with the jack of hearts. Declarer wins his ace, cashes his spades and plays a club. When you win your ace of clubs you will be able to cash the ten of hearts. The defence will make one more trick, declarer making three spades, two hearts, one diamond and three clubs, nine in all. Your lead, i.e. your attack on declarer, established one trick for you to cash together with your two aces and, eventually, the king of diamonds. Can you do better? Set up this same hand again and try opening leads from the other suits. We will have another look at the hand in the next lesson.

Lesson 17
MiniBridge 12

In the last lesson we defended this hand which South chose to play in no-trumps.

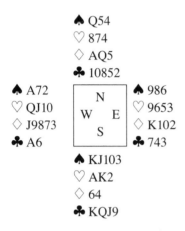

```
              ♠ Q54
              ♡ 874
              ◇ AQ5
              ♣ 10852
♠ A72      ┌─────────┐   ♠ 986
♡ QJ10     │   N     │   ♡ 9653
◇ J9873    │ W   E   │   ◇ K102
♣ A6       │   S     │   ♣ 743
           └─────────┘
              ♠ KJ103
              ♡ AK2
              ◇ 64
              ♣ KQJ9
```

On the queen of hearts lead, declarer made nine tricks, his goal with 25 points. Did you find a more punishing opening lead?

Let us see what happens on a diamond lead. Have you set out the hand so that you can follow it through?

On West's diamond lead declarer plays low from dummy. East wins the king and returns a diamond to dummy's queen. Declarer plays spades and you win to play another diamond to dummy's ace. Declarer cashes his spades and then plays a club, which you win and cash two diamond tricks.

This time you have made three diamond tricks and two black aces leaving declarer with just eight tricks, one short of his goal. But could you do better?

Suppose that you and your partner have agreed that you will lead the fourth highest card of your longest suit (i.e. the fourth down, counting from the top). Now, when you lead the seven of diamonds and declarer plays low from dummy, what should your partner do?

When you lead the seven, partner can work out that you must have three of the seven cards that are higher than the seven. That leaves four cards higher than the seven in the other three hands. He can see two of them in dummy, the ace and queen, and two in his own hand, the king and ten. So declarer does not have a card to beat the seven. Your partner plays the two of diamonds and your seven holds the trick. You continue with diamonds, the three, telling partner you had a five-card suit. Declarer plays the queen, but your partner wins with the king and returns his ten, knocking out dummy's ace.

When declarer plays spades you win and cash two diamonds. You will also make the ace of clubs. This time you made four diamond tricks together with two aces, holding declarer to seven tricks.

When you are defending against no-trumps you aim to establish tricks for the small cards in your longest suit, expecting your honours to make tricks in any event. Lead the fourth highest card from your longest suit unless it is headed by a three-card sequence in which case lead the top.

Lesson 18
MiniBridge 13

```
              ♠ Q54
              ♡ 874
              ◇ AQ5
              ♣ 10852
  ♠ A72       ┌─────────┐    ♠ 986
  ♡ QJ10      │    N    │    ♡ 9653
  ◇ J9873     │ W     E │    ◇ K102
  ♣ A6        │    S    │    ♣ 743
              └─────────┘
              ♠ KJ103
              ♡ AK2
              ◇ 64
              ♣ KQJ9
```

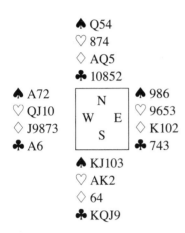

You saw this hand in the last lesson when West had to lead against a no-trump contract. Declarer made seven tricks on best defence after the seven of diamonds lead.

When you lead against a suit contract it is not particularly advantageous to lead your longest suit. When you have established your suit declarer will be able to trump your winners. You have to try to take tricks with high cards. If South decides to play in clubs rather than no-trumps then you should look to that favourite lead of the top card in a three-card sequence, the queen of hearts.

Do you remember why you lead the top card? If you don't remember, have a quick look back at Lesson 16.

Set up the hand and follow the play through. Declarer wins the queen of hearts with the king and plays the king of clubs. You win the ace and continue with the jack of hearts which declarer wins with the ace. He draws the defenders' trumps and plays a spade, which you win with the ace. You cash the ten of hearts and play a spade which declarer wins in hand. Although nine tricks, his goal, are secure, he would like to make as many tricks as possible.

He leads a diamond from his hand towards the ace-queen in dummy. He intends to play the queen of diamonds when you play low. This is known as a *finesse*. If you hold the king declarer will make the queen and then the ace, making in all ten tricks, three spades, two hearts, two diamonds and three clubs. On this occasion the queen of diamonds loses to the king and he makes only nine tricks.

Suppose the jack and king of diamonds are interchanged. Set out the hand again but change the East-West cards to:

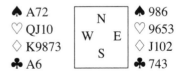

```
  ♠ A72       ┌─────────┐    ♠ 986
  ♡ QJ10      │    N    │    ♡ 9653
  ◇ K9873     │ W     E │    ◇ J102
  ♣ A6        │    S    │    ♣ 743
              └─────────┘
```

This time when declarer plays the queen of diamonds it holds the trick and he makes an extra trick. This was not for any reason of good or bad play but because of the position of the king of diamonds. Good play is not always winning play but gives you a better chance.

Lesson 19
MiniBridge 14

This is the hand we have been looking at over the past few lessons:

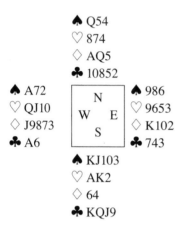

♠ Q54
♡ 874
◇ AQ5
♣ 10852

♠ A72
♡ QJ10
◇ J9873
♣ A6

N
W E
S

♠ 986
♡ 9653
◇ K102
♣ 743

♠ KJ103
♡ AK2
◇ 64
♣ KQJ9

You led the queen of hearts against a no-trump contract, but found this was not the best lead. Declarer won and played a spade, which you won to play another heart. It was not said which spade declarer played. If it had been the three it would have been an error for you to play the ace. On the actual hand it did not matter but what if declarer's hand had been:

♠ K863
♡ AK2
◇ 64
♣ KQJ9

Use a pack of cards to set up the hand with these cards as South (and your partner with

the J109 of spades). Now if you play the ace of spades when South leads one you set up the king and queen of spades as tricks for declarer. If you play low the queen will hold but when declarer plays another spade your partner plays the ten, which will hold if declarer ducks, while if he covers with the king you win with the ace. The highest spade is now partner's jack. You have made two spade tricks instead of the one that you made before.

There are at least two adages that cover this position: '*second hand low*' and '*aces are meant for kings*'. They both suggest that it is usually, but not always, better to use your aces and kings to capture declarer's high honours rather than his twos and threes.

This is an important principle to remember. Inexperienced players rush in with their high cards because they fear that if they don't take them immediately they will not make them later.

In the above example there is no need to worry. If dummy's queen holds the trick then declarer must have the king so you will surely make the trick later, perhaps with interest. Occasionally the trick does disappear but in the long run you will gain more often by playing low. It pays not to rush in with your honours unless you can see a certain way of defeating the contract.

Lesson 20
MiniBridge 15

In the last lesson we mentioned the adage: *'aces are meant for kings'*. This means that it is usually, but not always, better to use your aces and kings to capture declarer's high honours rather than his twos and threes.

There are exceptions to this advice. Set out the hand below and follow it through.

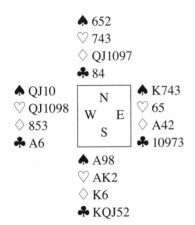

♠ 652
♡ 743
◇ QJ1097
♣ 84

♠ QJ10
♡ QJ1098
◇ 853
♣ A6

♠ K743
♡ 65
◇ A42
♣ 10973

♠ A98
♡ AK2
◇ K6
♣ KQJ52

South has chosen to play in no-trumps where his target is eight tricks with 23 points between the two hands.

Against a no-trump contract you lead the queen of hearts, not the nine. Remember that if your longest suit is headed by a three-card sequence you should lead the top card. Declarer wins with his king and hopes to make tricks with dummy's diamonds.

If he plays a low diamond first and a defender wins the ace, the presence of the king in declarer's hand *blocks* the suit and means he cannot cash all the diamond winners. However, if he leads the *king* and a defender wins the ace, he can reach dummy's diamond winners by playing his six. So at trick two, declarer plays the king of diamonds. What should your partner do?

He should duck this trick, i.e. let the king hold. When declarer plays another diamond what should your partner do this time?

He should win because he knows that declarer doesn't have another diamond to play. How does he know this? When declarer leads a suit, if you are not going to win the trick you should play your cards upwards to show an odd number of cards in the suit and play high-low with an even number. Here you play the three followed by the five of diamonds to show an odd number.

Having won the ace of diamonds your partner plays a heart which declarer wins with his king. He continues with the king of clubs, which you win with your ace. You cash your hearts and play the queen of spades. Declarer wins and cashes his top clubs but when the suit does not break 3-3 the defence makes the rest of the tricks. Declarer is two tricks short of his target – count them up.

If East wins the first diamond how many tricks does declarer make? If you play the hand through you should find that declarer would make eight tricks.

Lesson 21
MiniBridge 16

When we began the series on MiniBridge, we were concerned only with playing to make as many tricks as possible. After a few articles we introduced the concept of targets which suggested the number of tricks to aim for depending on the combined point-count of the declaring side (see Lesson 11).

There was no judgement involved in selecting these targets, rather they were thrust willy-nilly upon the hapless declarer. In bridge and for the next stage of MiniBridge that is not the case. In bridge the bidding determines the precise number of tricks that declarer has to make whilst in MiniBridge the declarer must decide for himself, in a limited way, how many tricks he wishes to aim for. Consider the hand below; set up the North-South cards as you wish except both hearts and clubs are to divide 3-2 and spades are to divide 4-4.

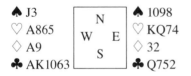

♠ J3
♡ A865
◇ A9
♣ AK1063

N
W   E
S

♠ 1098
♡ KQ74
◇ 32
♣ Q752

Play through the hand and decide how many tricks you would make with clubs as trumps, with hearts as trumps and at no-trumps.

The score for a successful contract generally depends upon two things, the *denomination* (the trump suit, or no-trumps) and the *level* (the number of tricks aimed for). In this lesson we will consider the denomination. The declaring side, which in MiniBridge always has more points than the defending side, should always expect to make more than half the tricks. Thus the declaring side scores only for the number of tricks it wins above six.

On the above hand with clubs as trumps you should make ten tricks: five trumps, four hearts and one diamond. Clubs and diamonds are known as the minor suits and each trick above six is worth 20 points. Thus ten tricks in clubs scores 80 points (4x20).

With hearts as trumps you should make eleven tricks. Did you? Hearts and spades are known as the major suits and they score 30 points for each trick above six. Thus eleven tricks with hearts as trumps scores 150 (5x30).

In no-trumps you should make nine tricks but here the scoring is a little more complicated. You score 40 points for the first trick over six and 30 points for each subsequent trick. Thus here you would score 100 points (40+30+30).

Lesson 22
MiniBridge 17

Should your play of the hand result in a score of 100 points or more it is referred to as a 'game' and you receive a bonus of 300 points. There is one small snag. To receive this bonus you must declare that you will make a game contract before the play starts. A game contract is eleven tricks in a minor (5x20=100), ten tricks in a major (4x30=120) or nine tricks in no-trumps (40+30+30=100). To make game in no-trumps requires only nine tricks – less than any other game contract. It is therefore a popular game to contract for.

Anything that scores less than 100 points is known as a partscore and receives a bonus of 50 points.

On this hand, you, West, are the dealer. You announce your 15 points, North has 3, East has 8 and South the remaining 14. Consider how many tricks you would expect to make:

♠ K82	N	♠ 973
♡ K97	W E	♡ QJ6543
◇ AJ3	S	◇ KQ72
♣ KJ98		♣ none

You decide that it is best to play in hearts and that you will lose three spade tricks if North has the ace, and a further trick to the ace of trumps. Thus you say that you will make a partscore in hearts. If you make nine tricks you will score 140 points (3x30+50bonus=140). If you make ten tricks you will score 170 points (4x30+50=170).

You have forgotten something – South said he had 14 points and North 3.

What are North's 3 points? South must have the ace of spades. You can therefore make your king of spades for one spade, five hearts and four diamonds ten tricks in all. Try it.

You could therefore have chosen game in hearts as your contract and would have scored the same 120 (4x30) points. However, in addition you would have had a bonus of 300 points for contracting and making a game, giving a total of 420 points – a much better score and why sometimes you must take a risk in deciding whether or not to go for game.

If you are to receive a bonus when you make your contract (either 50 or 300 points), it will come as no surprise to learn that there are penalties when you fail. If you play in a partscore then you lose 50 points for each trick fewer than seven that you make; if you play in game you lose 50 points for each trick by which you fail. So, for example, if you contract for game in diamonds (eleven tricks) and make eight tricks then you score minus 150 (3x50=150).

Lesson 23
MiniBridge 18

We shall finish off this MiniBridge section by giving you some problems to see how well you have understood the previous articles. Try not to look at the full hand until you have worked out what you would do.

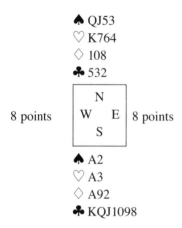

♠ QJ53
♡ K764
◇ 108
♣ 532

8 points | N W E S | 8 points

♠ A2
♡ A3
◇ A92
♣ KQJ1098

You have chosen to contract for game in no-trumps (nine tricks), hoping to make five tricks in clubs (once you have knocked out the ace), the ace and king of hearts and the aces of spades and diamonds.

West leads the six of diamonds which goes to East's queen. How would you play?

Unluckily the defenders have found the best lead. You will be all right if the diamonds divide 4-4, but if they are 5-3 or 6-2, when a defender wins his ace of clubs they will be able to take enough diamond tricks to sink your contract. Can you see a possible solution?

If the defender who holds the ace of clubs has fewer than four diamonds you can still succeed. *Duck* (i.e. don't win) the first diamond trick. Best is for the defence to continue with another diamond but you play low on this trick as well. Win the third diamond and play the king of clubs. This time you are in luck and will still make your contract. The full deal is:

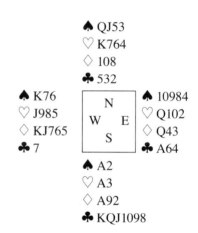

♠ QJ53
♡ K764
◇ 108
♣ 532

♠ K76   ♠ 10984
♡ J985   N   ♡ Q102
◇ KJ765 W E ◇ Q43
♣ 7   S   ♣ A64

♠ A2
♡ A3
◇ A92
♣ KQJ1098

Lesson 24
MiniBridge 19

When you feel you have mastered the idea of choosing your denomination and whether or not you want to go for the game bonus, you can add a further target to your MiniBridge game, which is one that also occurs in Bridge proper. It is the most exciting contract in the game and is called a *slam*. If you contract to make a small slam, you are proposing that you will make twelve of the thirteen available tricks (a grand slam is all thirteen tricks). The total bonus for bidding and making a slam is 800 points (including the 300 game bonus). Try your hand at the following problem.

♠ 9874
♡ QJ
◇ AK5
♣ AQ93

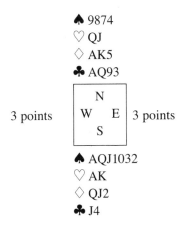

3 points

3 points

♠ AQJ1032
♡ AK
◇ QJ2
♣ J4

With 34 points between your two hands you decided to try for slam in spades. If either black-suit king is well placed you should make your slam without difficulty.

West leads the six of diamonds. How should you play?

This hand is a lot easier to play at MiniBridge than it would be at bridge. At MiniBridge you know that each opponent has a black-suit king because you know that each has 3 points. If you start by taking a trump finesse and it loses you know you will go down because you know that East will hold the king of clubs.

Best is to start by playing on clubs. If the club finesse works you will make all thirteen tricks because East will hold the king of spades. But if the club finesse loses to East's king you know that West will hold the king of spades. So you don't take the spade finesse; cash the ace instead and hope it is a singleton – your only hope. Play the hand through and try it.

This is the full deal:

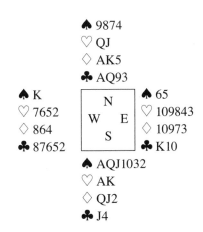

♠ 9874
♡ QJ
◇ AK5
♣ AQ93

♠ K
♡ 7652
◇ 864
♣ 87652

♠ 65
♡ 109843
◇ 10973
♣ K10

♠ AQJ1032
♡ AK
◇ QJ2
♣ J4

Lesson 25
MiniBridge 20

It is not only declarer who can use the information about everyone's high-card strength. Look at this problem:

You are dealt the following hand as West:

♠ QJ1098
♡ QJ
♢ 7
♣ KQ763

Although your hand is quite promising, South becomes declarer because the high-card points are distributed:

```
              10 points
              ┌──────────┐
  11 points   │          │  4 points
              └──────────┘
              15 points
```

North puts down his hand:

♠ 543
♡ 8
♢ AKQJ109
♣ 1054

South chooses to play in game in No-Trumps (nine tricks).

What do you lead?

This is another occasion where it is easier to know what to do at MiniBridge than it would be at bridge proper where you have to make your lead before seeing the dummy.

You wouldn't know, as you do here, that declarer has nine tricks: six diamonds, two aces and the king in one of the major suits (spades or hearts).

It is vital that you take five tricks immediately. As your partner has only 4 points, you have to hope that he has the ace of clubs. So, the answer is to lead a low club (your fourth highest, the five, is the normal choice – see Lesson 17).

This is the full deal:

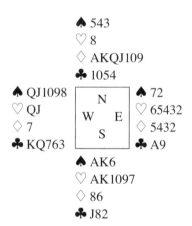

```
                    ♠ 543
                    ♡ 8
                    ♢ AKQJ109
                    ♣ 1054
      ♠ QJ1098    ┌──────┐    ♠ 72
      ♡ QJ        │  N   │    ♡ 65432
      ♢ 7         │ W  E │    ♢ 5432
      ♣ KQ763     │  S   │    ♣ A9
                  └──────┘
                    ♠ AK6
                    ♡ AK1097
                    ♢ 86
                    ♣ J82
```

Although South was unsuccessful in his attempt to make game, he was correct to try to do so. Had the opposing clubs been divided 4-3 (which is more likely than the 5-2 break that actually occurred) he would have succeeded. He would also have succeeded on other occasions when it was not so obvious to lead a club from your hand.

Part II
Basic Bidding

Now you can play the cards with some degree of confidence, it is time to introduce you to bidding. But don't worry, there will be plenty of opportunities to put your card-playing skills into practice.

Lesson 26
Bidding basics 1

To remind you of what we said right at the beginning of this book, there are two phases of bridge: first the *bidding* and then the *play*. The reason we have concentrated on explaining what happens in the play via MiniBridge is that it is difficult to understand the bidding until you see the purpose of it. In the MiniBridge section you have seen the idea of 'targets' – when as declarer you see the dummy, not only do you decide what *denomination* to play in, but you also estimate how many tricks you think you might make.

Now that we are switching to bridge proper, you will find that the phase called *bidding* is all about setting up the *denomination* and the *targets*, but by an entirely new process, the *auction*.

The auction

The auction consists of a series of *calls*. The two types of call we consider here are *bids* and *pass* (later we will look at *doubles* and *redoubles*). As in a commercial auction, each new bid has to be higher than the previous one.

As in MiniBridge, North-South and East-West are partners in the bidding. Unlike in a commercial auction, a player is allowed to bid only when it is his or her turn.

A bid consists of a *number* and a *denomination* (suit or no-trumps). Here is how auctions are displayed:

South	West	North	East
1♡	1♠	Pass	2♠
Pass	Pass	Pass	

The dealer in this case is South, and he starts the bidding with One Heart. West overcalls with One Spade. Why is that a higher bid than One Heart? We will explain in the next lesson.

North passes. That is, he does not want to make a bid. East now bids Two Spades, and no-one else wants to bid again. An auction ends when there are three consecutive passes. The last bid becomes the *final contract*.

What does a bid mean?

The *number* part of a bid refers to the number of tricks you aim to win above six, and the *denomination* is your suggested trump suit, or no-trumps. So, for example, to bid Four Spades means that you expect to make ten tricks with spades as trumps.

There are 35 bids in all – one for each suit and one for no-trumps at the levels of one to seven. Whoever has made the highest bid at the end of auction 'buys' the contract, just as if you were bidding for a Picasso.

Lesson 27
Bidding basics 2

One further idea it is vital to grasp is that the *rank* of the suits becomes important.

The auction continues

We mentioned in Lesson 2 that bridge hands are always written down in the same sequence. The order of the suits, starting with the lowest, is clubs, diamonds, hearts, spades, no-trumps. One useful tip is that the order of the suits is alphabetical. In an auction, if you wish to bid a lower-ranking suit than the one bid previously you have to bid it at a higher level. For example, suppose your right-hand opponent has bid One Heart (seven tricks in hearts). With spades you can say *One* Spade because spades rank higher than hearts, but with diamonds you have to bid *Two* Diamonds because they rank lower than hearts.

Last week we looked at one simple auction. Here is another:

South	West	North	East
1♡	1♠	2♢	2♠
3♢	Pass	Pass	Pass

Here South, the dealer, started the ball rolling with One Heart, i.e. he contracted to make seven tricks with hearts as trumps. West bid One Spade. Because spades rank higher than hearts he did not have to go up a level. In order to introduce his diamond suit, North had to 'raise the level', bidding Two Diamonds. East had a hand that was good enough to think his side could make eight tricks with spades as trumps if his partner thought he could make seven so he bid Two Spades. South had support for North's diamonds, and in order to express this had to go to the three level, as diamonds are lower ranking than spades. Nobody had anything else to say after South's Three Diamonds, so they all passed. North 'bought' the hand in a final contract of Three Diamonds. Although it was South who bid Three Diamonds, North bid the suit first. North's aim is to make nine tricks with diamonds as trumps.

The opening lead

The player on declarer's left (in this case East) makes his opening lead and *only then does South put down his hand*, the dummy. Note the significant departure from MiniBridge, where the opening lead is made after dummy has been revealed and the contract decided.

Lesson 28
Opening the bidding

After you have picked up your hand and sorted it into suits, you should count your points (which in future will be referred to as HCP – High Card Points). You do this in just the same way as you did in MiniBridge. Since there are 40 points in the pack, your fair share of points is 10 and you need just a little more than that, say 12, to start the auction – or *open the bidding*. If you have fewer than 12 you begin with a pass.

The general rule, if you have a five-card or longer suit, is that you open the bidding with One of your longest suit.

(A)♠ AQ652	(B)♠ 5
♡ K754	♡ AKJ1076
♢ 65	♢ AQ2
♣ A5	♣ 762

Since you have more than 12 points, with Hand (A), you open One Spade and with Hand (B) you open One Heart .

However, the most frequent hand-type you will be dealt is one that has the cards distributed more evenly among the four suits, i.e. a more balanced hand, such as:

(C)♠ AQ6	(D)♠ 543
♡ K754	♡ AKJ10
♢ 6532	♢ AQ2
♣ A5	♣ 762

(E)♠ 862	(F)♠ AQ3
♡ 75	♡ A1092
♢ KQJ104	♢ KJ64
♣ AK6	♣ Q7

It is extremely important concept to understand the difference between *balanced* and *unbalanced* hands. If you and your partner do not share an eight-card (minimum) trump suit, you have already learned that you should usually declare in no-trumps. Balanced hands tend to play better in no-trumps, whereas unbalanced hands usually fare better in a suit contract. A rule-of-thumb definition of a balanced hand is: *no void, no singleton and not more than one doubleton* (i.e. no suit with no or one card, no more than one suit with only two cards). So Hand (E), even though it has a five-card suit, falls into the definition of a balanced hand.

Think about the shape of a balanced hand. If you hold five spades and four hearts in a hand, can it be balanced? See Hand (A). Within your hand of thirteen cards, you hold nine cards in two suits, so your other two suits can only be distributed 2-2 or 3-1, and in either case you break the definition.

Most learners find it easier to start by learning about bidding in no-trumps because the bids are clearly defined and limit the HCP value of the hand. A useful guideline is: *if your hand is balanced you should bid no-trumps at the earliest truthful opportunity.*

Lesson 29
Opening One No-Trump

You will learn in this book to open One No-Trump with a balanced hand of 12–14 HCP. (This is not a rule of bridge. You will meet players who open One No-Trump to show 15–17 HCP or 16–18. However, 12–14 is the most commonly played in this country.) In a future lesson we will look at the situation where you have more than 14 HCP; of course, if you have fewer than 12 you pass.

Make up the following hand, which is a typical One No-Trump opening:

♠	K74
♡	Q93
◇	AJ86
♣	K65

It is perfectly balanced with 13 HCP. If you remove the king of clubs and replace it with the king of hearts, is the hand still balanced?

♠	K74
♡	KQ93
◇	AJ86
♣	65

Your club suit would then be very weak, but you are not promising good cards in every suit (how could you with only 12–14 HCP?), so this is still a One No-Trump opening.

Make up the following hands and decide if you would open One No-Trump (see end of page for answer).

(A) ♠ K654
　　♡ A2
　　◇ QJ64
　　♣ Q75

(B) ♠ K543
　　♡ A765
　　◇ QJ64
　　♣ K

(C) ♠ 762
　　♡ KQ32
　　◇ AJ5
　　♣ Q76

(D) ♠ KQ4
　　♡ 87654
　　◇ AKJ7
　　♣ 10

(E) ♠ A63
　　♡ A102
　　◇ KQJ54
　　♣ 62

(F) ♠ KQ2
　　♡ KQ5
　　◇ AJ54
　　♣ J72

The great advantage of opening One No-Trump, which describes the nature and strength of your hand within narrow limits, is that it frequently allows *responder* (i.e. the partner of the opening bidder) to decide the final contract immediately. There are only two reasons for responder bidding on over a One No-Trump opening. The first is because he thinks game might be on, and the second is because he has a weak unbalanced hand and thinks it will be better to play in a suit contract.

Of the hands given above, (A), (C) and (E) are One No-Trump openers. Hands (B) and (D) are unsuitable because they contain a singleton. Hand (F) is unsuitable because it is too strong – remember a One No-Trump opening shows 12–14 HCP.

Lesson 30
Responding to One No-Trump

We will start by looking at the case where responder has a balanced hand. In Lesson 22 we said that a game in no-trumps means making nine tricks and in Lesson 11, where we looked at targets for MiniBridge, we suggested you set a target of nine tricks when the combined hands held 25–26. So, if responder has a balanced hand and knows that his side has at least 25 points he goes straight to game, i.e. if he has 13 or more points he bids Three No-Trumps. On the other hand, if he knows that his side cannot have 25 points, he passes, i.e. if he has 10 or fewer HCP he simply lets his partner declare One No-Trump. If he has 11 or 12 HCP he needs to consult his partner to find out if he is maximum or minimum. He does this by making an *invitational* bid of Two No-Trumps. Over Two No-Trumps, the opener passes with 12, bids Three No-Trumps with 14 and tosses a mental coin if he has 13.

How would you respond to partner's One No-Trump opening with the following hands:

(A) ♠ AQ5　　　(B) ♠ KJ2
　　♡ KJ72　　　　♡ 874
　　♢ K984　　　　♢ A72
　　♣ 62　　　　　♣ Q983

(C) ♠ KJ105　　(D) ♠ K64
　　♡ AQ72　　　　♡ A982
　　♢ 1094　　　　♢ KQ4
　　♣ J3　　　　　♣ AQ4

These are simply a matter of addition. Bid Three No-Trumps with (A), pass with (B) and bid Two No-Trumps with (C). With Hand (D) bid Three No-Trumps. Although you are very strong, the maximum your partnership can hold is 32 which is not usually enough for Six No-Trumps (as in MiniBridge you generally need 33 points for a small slam in no-trumps – see Lesson 11). Bid Three No-Trumps.

Where unbalanced hands are concerned you must choose between making a simple bid or a jump bid in a new suit.

(E) ♠ 764　　　　(F) ♠ KQJ105
　　♡ QJ972　　　　♡ A53
　　♢ J1076　　　　♢ 7
　　♣ 5　　　　　　♣ AJ107

Bid Two Hearts with Hand (E). This is a weakness take-out which partner must pass. You are bidding not necessarily because you expect to make your contract, but because you hope to do better than partner would in no-trumps.

With a strong unbalanced hand jump a level in your longest suit. This asks partner to choose between game in your suit and game in no-trumps. With Hand (F) jump to Three Spades. This is *forcing*. A forcing bid is one which partner is not permitted to pass (by partnership agreement, not the laws of bridge).

Lesson 31
More on responding to One No-Trump

In order to test your understanding of what we covered in the last lesson, how would you respond to partner's One No-Trump with the following hands?

(A) ♠ 5
♡ KQJ83
♢ K762
♣ 872

(B) ♠ AQ3
♡ K1065
♢ Q1065
♣ 54

Even though Hand (A) is considerably stronger than Hand (E) in the last lesson, it is still worth only Two Hearts. Your side has a maximum of only 23 HCP which, more often than not, won't be enough for game.

With Hand (B) you have a balanced 11 HCP. Bid an invitational Two No-Trumps, asking partner to bid game if he is maximum.

(C) ♠ KQJ1085
♡ A5
♢ Q62
♣ 82

(D) ♠ KJ763
♡ A6
♢ Q1076
♣ A5

With Hand (C) you have enough for game, no real interest in a slam and a good strong suit of your own. Bid Four Spades straight away.

You have enough for game on Hand (D) but you don't know about partner's spade support. Bid Three Spades. This is a forcing bid so partner must not pass. If he has three or more spades he will raise you to Four Spades; if he has only two he will bid Three No-Trumps and you will pass.

(E) ♠ A3
♡ KJ5
♢ QJ1076
♣ K54

(F) ♠ 5
♡ AQ64
♢ AKJ1065
♣ Q5

On Hand (E) you have enough for a game. When your five-card suit is a minor it is rarely right to bid it when you have a balanced hand. To make a game in diamonds you need to make eleven tricks and the nine you need for no-trumps is usually much easier. Go straight to Three No-Trumps.

Hand (F) is more challenging. Here you have 16 HCP and some powerful distribution. A slam could easily be on. Jump to Three Diamonds, forcing partner to bid again. You may find an eight-card heart fit as he will bid a four-card major if he has one, otherwise he will bid Three No-Trumps or raise diamonds if he has a fit.

We have covered a lot of ground in the last few lessons and now it is time for some practice. Get out a pack of cards, make yourself up a typical One No-Trump opener and deal the other cards randomly into the other three hands. Work out what you would respond to the One No-Trump opening with each of the other three hands.

Lesson 32
Stronger balanced hands

If you have a balanced hand but are too strong to open One No-Trump, then you should open One of your longest suit and rebid in no-trumps at your first opportunity. With a 4-3-3-3 or 5-3-3-2 distribution this is easy because you have only one 'longest' suit. If you have two four-card suits it is not quite so straightforward.

If the partnership has an eight-card major-suit fit it is usually a good idea to play in it, otherwise no-trumps will normally be right. The easiest way to find a major-suit fit is to open a major so, with a four-card major and a four-card minor, it is better to open the major. If you have both majors you should open One Heart. If partner has four spades he will usually bid the suit so the spade fit will be found. The choice with both minors is less important because the hand will probably be played in no-trumps in any event, but this course recommends One Diamond.

Having opened One of your longest suit and heard partner's response in a new suit, you rebid no-trumps at the lowest possible level with 15–17 HCP and make a jump rebid in No-Trumps with 18–19 HCP. If you are lucky enough to be dealt 20–22 HCP you open Two No-Trumps in the first place, but more of that, and even stronger hands, later.

Choose your opening bid (and rebid) with the following hands:

(A) ♠ AK75
   ♡ AQ54
   ◇ K5
   ♣ 873

(B) ♠ AQ43
   ♡ 64
   ◇ AQ6
   ♣ K1065

(C) ♠ A65
   ♡ KJ104
   ◇ AQ65
   ♣ A6

(D) ♠ AQ3
   ♡ KJ1054
   ◇ A3
   ♣ Q53

Hand (A) has 16 HCP and is 4-4 in the majors. Open One Heart. If partner responds One Spade give a jump raise to Three Spades (more on this later), but if he bids a new suit at the two level, rebid Two No-Trumps.

Hand (B) has 15 HCP and 4-4 in the black suits. Open One Spade. If partner bids a new suit at the two level rebid Two No-Trumps.

Hand (C) has 18 HCP and is 4-4 in the red suits. Open One Heart. If partner bids One Spade jump to Two No-Trumps; if he bids a new suit at the two level bid Three No-Trumps.

With Hand (D) it is clear to open One Heart. Make a simple rebid in no-trumps if partner makes a change-of-suit response. If partner has three-card support for hearts he will be able to show that on the next round and the eight-card fit won't be lost.

Lesson 33
Putting it into practice

The time has come for a full hand.

You pick up as South:

♠	AQ
♡	K432
◇	AJ105
♣	J73

You count up your points: 15 – too many for One No-Trump. When you have a balanced hand too strong for One No-Trump you choose a four-card major if possible, so here you open One Heart. Your partner responds Two Clubs, showing at least four clubs and at least 9 HCP (more on that later). So you rebid Two No-Trumps, showing 15–17 HCP, and your partner raises you to Three No-Trumps.

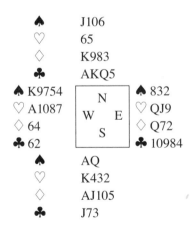

♠	J106
♡	65
◇	K983
♣	AKQ5

♠ K9754	♠ 832
♡ A1087	♡ QJ9
◇ 64	◇ Q72
♣ 62	♣ 10984

♠	AQ
♡	K432
◇	AJ105
♣	J73

Contract: Three No-Trumps by South
Lead: five of spades

Count your tricks. You have two spades, two diamonds and four clubs, eight in all.

Where is your ninth trick to come from? The answer to that is from diamonds. You may not have to lose a trick to the queen of diamonds but even if you do you will then have established an extra diamond trick for your contract.

What can go wrong? If East gains the lead he may play a high heart through your king and if the suit is distributed as above you will lose four tricks in the suit and go one down.

What can you do about it? You can make sure you don't lose a trick to East.

Win the queen of spades. Play a diamond to dummy's king and a diamond back to your jack. If West were to win this trick the defenders would be unable to take four more tricks immediately and as soon as you gained the lead you would take nine.

Lesson 34
Opening one of a suit

There is a fundamental difference between opening One No-Trump as opposed to One of a Suit. A One No-Trump opening bid is a *limit bid*. A limit bid defines a hand within narrow limits. Here One No-Trump shows a balanced hand within a 3-point range. No-trump bids are by nature limit bids at all levels – they tell almost everything about the hand in *one bid*.

We are now moving into the more sophisticated area of bidding *unbalanced* hands, which invariably require more than one bid to describe their shape and HCP strength.

Consider the best possible hand with which to make thirteen tricks in no-trumps: the ace, king, queen in all suits, plus a jack. 37 HCP. But what is the best possible hand in a suit contract? Thirteen spades, of course. Only 10 HCP. This contrast demonstrates the value of long suits, which can be more valuable than HCP.

Having acquired your basic no-trump bidding skills, it is now vital to realise that when you open One of a Suit the only message you are sending to partner is, 'I have at least four cards in this suit and enough HCP (usually 12+) to open the bidding.' You will need to hear partner's *response* to enable you to make your *rebid*, which will define the shape and strength of your hand further.

When you open the bidding with One of a Suit you are promising partner that if he makes a forcing response you will make a rebid which will give more information

about your hand. You may make your rebid in no-trumps (see Lesson 32) promising a balanced hand too strong for an opening One No-Trump. If your hand is unbalanced you will make your rebid either in another suit (maybe supporting partner) or at a higher level in your first suit. We will look at rebids in more detail in a later article but when you open with One of a Suit you should have already planned your *rebid*.

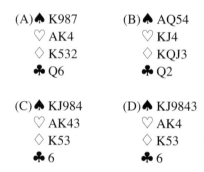

You should open One Spade with all four of the above hands. On Hand (A) you intend to pass a One No-Trump or Two Spade response or rebid Two No-Trumps over a two-level response in a new suit, showing a balanced 15–17. On Hand (B) you will rebid Two No-Trumps over One No-Trump or Two Spades, but will need to jump to Three No-Trumps to show 18–19 if partner responds at the two level. On Hand (C) you intend to rebid your second suit, hearts, and on Hand (D) you will rebid your six-card spade suit.

Lesson 35
Opening with an unbalanced hand

Do you remember the definition of a balanced hand? *No void, no singleton and not more than one doubleton.*

Choosing your opening bid can be easier when you are unbalanced. Again, you count your points. If you have 12 or more you simply open One of your longest suit.

The only problem is when you have two five-card suits. Here the answer is straightforward: open the higher ranking. It is easy to see why this should be so when you hold touching suits: you can next bid your lower-ranking one and partner can choose between your suits at the same level. Suppose you hold five spades and five hearts. If you open One Spade and then bid Two Hearts over partner's One No-Trump response, he can pass if he prefers hearts and bid Two Spades if he prefers spades. If you opened One Heart and rebid Two Spades he would have to go to Three Hearts if he preferred that suit. When you have a major suit and a minor suit it is always preferable to bid the major suit first.

Choose your opening bid with the following hands:

(A) ♠ 5
♡ AKQ32
♢ 1098
♣ A432

(B) ♠ J9875
♡ AKQ2
♢ K5
♣ 63

With Hand (A) open One Heart, which happens to be your strongest as well as your longest suit. On Hand (B) you should open One Spade. Even though the suit is weak it is the length that counts.

(C) ♠ 5
♡ AKQ3
♢ 109854
♣ A63

(D) ♠ KJ1076
♡ A54
♢ QJ4
♣ Q6

On Hand (C) you again open in your longest suit, this time One Diamond. A long time ago it was fashionable to open One Heart with this hand but don't listen to anyone who tells you that now.

Hand (D) is interesting. It falls into our definition of a balanced hand but this time the five-card suit is a major. In this course we are going to suggest that you open One No-Trump on 5-3-3-2 hands even when the five-card suit is a major. However, this is not a universal approach and you will surely find some people who disagree.

(E) ♠ KJ107
♡ A5
♢ QJ432
♣ Q6

(F) ♠ 65
♡ AK763
♢ KQ874
♣ 3

Don't be tempted to open One No-Trump on Hand (E). Its two doubletons make it an unbalanced hand. Open One Diamond, your longest suit. On Hand (F) open One Heart, the higher-ranking of two five-card suits.

Lesson 36
Raising partner

Now it is time to look at the action from responder's point of view. Partner opens the bidding; how should you respond?

We have mentioned before that the purpose of bidding is to decide on both the *denomination* and the *level* of the final contract. If you have good support for the suit partner has opened you already know what the final denomination should be – his suit. Tell him so by raising his suit. In a major suit you are looking for an eight-card fit; since partner needs four to open, you need four to support him.

Whenever you have four-card support for partner's major you should always raise his suit immediately*

When you raise partner's suit you are defining your hand quite precisely in one bid – it is another example of a *limit bid*. With 6–8 HCP you make a single raise; with 9–11 you make a jump raise; and with 12–14 you make a double jump raise.

What do you respond to your partner's One Spade opening with the following hands:

(A) ♠ K765	(B) ♠ A876
♡ K542	♡ 65
◇ 62	◇ QJ76
♣ 876	♣ K53

Hand (A) is a minimum raise to Two Spades. Hand (B) is an ace stronger and you should tell partner so by jumping to Three Spades.

(C) ♠ 8743	(D) ♠ AQ3
♡ AKJ105	♡ 8765
◇ 76	◇ J76
♣ Q6	♣ J53

Inexperienced players often make the mistake of bidding hearts on Hand (C). When you have already found one eight-card major-suit fit there is no need to look for another. Bid Three Spades. If you respond Two Hearts partner will never believe you hold four spades with him.

Although your spades are very strong on Hand (D), there is no reason to suppose partner has five cards in the suit. Respond One No-Trump (more of that later).

(E) ♠ AQ65	(F) ♠ J8754
♡ K63	♡ 6
◇ A876	◇ AK65
♣ 63	♣ 874

With Hand (E) you have enough for game (13+12=25). Go all the way to Four Spades.

On Hand (F) you should respond Three Spades. Although you have only 8 HCP you are too good for a raise to Two Spades. There are several reasons for upgrading this hand: (1) you have *five*-card trump support, (2) you have a singleton, and (3) you have a powerful ace-king combination in a side suit.

*There are some exceptions to this when you are very strong which we will deal with later (see Lesson 156).

42

Lesson 37
Putting it into practice

You pick up as South:

South	West	North	East
1♠	Pass	3♠	Pass
4♠	All Pass		

♠   Q8732
♡   AK42
◇   KQ
♣   75

Contract: Four Spades by South
Lead: king of clubs

You open One Spade, your left-hand opponent (LHO) passes and your partner raises to Three Spades. RHO passes and it is up to you. Do you pass or press on to game?

There are two aspects of this hand that lift it into the above-minimum category: (1) you have 14 HCP, a couple more than necessary; and (2) you have 5-4-2-2 distribution which is usually worth a little more than 5-3-3-2. So you bid Four Spades.

West leads the king of clubs and this is the full deal:

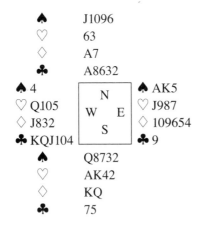

    ♠   J1096
    ♡   63
    ◇   A7
    ♣   A8632

♠ 4   ♠ AK5
♡ Q105   ♡ J987
◇ J832   ◇ 109654
♣ KQJ104 ♣ 9

    ♠   Q8732
    ♡   AK42
    ◇   KQ
    ♣   75

Count your tricks. You have three in spades (once you have knocked out the ace and king), two in hearts, two in diamonds and one in clubs, eight in all.

Where are the other two to come from? The club suit is a possibility if it breaks 3-3, but a much better chance is to ruff two hearts in the dummy.

What can go wrong? If trumps break 2-2 there will be no problems. After you have finished drawing trumps there will still be two left in dummy with which to ruff hearts. But if trumps breaks 3-1, as here, East will play the king, ace and another trump and now you will have only one trump left in dummy. You still have the chance of a 3-3 club break but when that fails to materialise you will go one down.

The solution is not difficult. You must ruff your hearts in the dummy *before* touching trumps. Win the ace of clubs, cash the ace and king of hearts and ruff a heart. Play a diamond back to your king and ruff your last heart. Now play a trump. All the defence will make are the ace and king of trumps and a club trick.

Lesson 38
Responding one of a suit

As we have said before, one of the many purposes of bidding is to discover if there is an eight-card major-suit fit. Consequently, all you need to respond One of a major to partner's opening is at least four cards in the suit and 6 or more HCP.

Why 6 HCP? Well, with 20 or more HCP partner would usually open at the two level (as we will see in a later article). So, the normal maximum for a one-level opening bid is about 19 HCP. You generally need about 25 HCP between your two hands for game, therefore you should respond with 6 HCP (in case partner has 19) but usually pass with fewer than that.

When you are very weak, it is sensible simply to let partner play the hand at the one level in his best suit, for if you force the auction higher you are more likely to go down in whatever contract you eventually settle.

What do you respond to a One Diamond opening bid with the following hands:

(A) ♠ KQJ5   (B) ♠ AQ4
    ♡ 874   ♡ J873
    ◇ 532   ◇ 87
    ♣ K65   ♣ Q1065

With Hands (A) and (B) it is quite straightforward. In both instances you have a four-card major, so bid it. It doesn't matter if it is a strong one as on Hand (A) or a weak one as on Hand (B).

(C) ♠ KJ76   (D) ♠ KJ1065
    ♡ KJ76   ♡ 874
    ◇ 65   ◇ 532
    ♣ 874   ♣ Q5

With both majors, as in Hand (C), bid the lower, One Heart. If partner has a four-card spade suit he will bid it and the fit will be found on the next round.

Just because a bid needs only four cards doesn't mean you have to bid something else with more. Respond One Spade on Hand (D).

(E) ♠ AQJ4   (F) ♠ 10872
    ♡ 762   ♡ 762
    ◇ 10872   ◇ AQJ4
    ♣ 63   ♣ 63

Hands (E) and (F) raise a point which, in my view, is often misunderstood even by quite good players. When you have support for partner's minor suit you should use your common sense. By all means bid a good four-card major such as on Hand (E), but when your major is poor and your support good, as on Hand (F), just raise partner immediately. After all, if he has a good hand and wants to proceed he can always introduce a four-card spade suit if he has one.

Lesson 39
No-trump responses

Sometimes you don't have a four-card major to bid at the one level and must look for an alternative. A One No-Trump response shows 6–9 HCP and denies an intervening major suit of four cards or more.

Here are some examples of a One No-Trump response to a One Heart opening:

(A) ♠ Q103　　(B) ♠ 65
　　♡ 762　　　　♡ 62
　　♢ AQ5　　　　♢ Q9863
　　♣ 9854　　　　♣ A1054

(C) ♠ KJ5　　(D) ♠ J42
　　♡ 3　　　　　♡ 73
　　♢ QJ743　　　♢ KQJ652
　　♣ J1087　　　♣ 76

Hand (A) is a perfect One No-Trump response, completely balanced with 8 HCP. If partner rebids in a suit to show an unbalanced hand you will know he has five or more hearts and that you have at least an eight-card fit there.

Hand (B) is a minimum with 6 HCP. Don't worry that you have just two little spades. A One No-Trump response doesn't promise stoppers in all the other suits.

Hand (C) is a maximum. Don't worry about holding a singleton heart. A One No-Trump response doesn't promise a balanced hand.

If may be tempting to bid Two Diamonds on Hand (D) with such a good suit, but you are not strong enough. As you will discover in the next lesson, you need at least 9 HCP to respond at the two level. Here bid One No-Trump; you may be able to bid your diamonds later.

What would you bid on the following hands after the One Heart opening?

(E) ♠ KJ4　　(F) ♠ AQ65
　　♡ 874　　　　♡ 872
　　♢ AJ105　　　♢ Q106
　　♣ Q106　　　♣ K107

You will notice that both these hands are too strong for a One No-Trump response. With Hand (E) respond Two No-Trumps, showing 11–12 HCP and a balanced hand. If you had a queen or a king more, you would jump to Three No-Trumps, showing 13–15 HCP. This balanced hand should not contain a four-card spade suit, though, so with Hand (F) you are better to start with One Spade.

Note that Hand (E) contains three-card support for hearts. After this jump to Two No-Trumps (or Three No-Trumps) partner, with a five-card major, needs to know whether to choose his suit or no-trumps as the final denomination. He cannot do this very easily unless he knows how many hearts you have, so it is best to have the agreement that these jumps show three cards in the suit opened.

Lesson 40
Responding two of a suit

The responding hands we are left with are hands of 10 or more HCP (or 9 with a five-card suit) without a suit that can be bid conveniently at the one level.

What do you respond to One Heart with these hands?

(A) ♠ A43　　　(B) ♠ K43
　　 ♡ 87　　　　　 ♡ 98
　　 ◇ AK763　　　 ◇ QJ65
　　 ♣ 964　　　　 ♣ A1065

With Hand (A) there is no problem. You have enough for a two-level response and one good five-card suit. Simply respond Two Diamonds.

With Hand (B), even though you have a balanced hand with no five-card suit, you are too strong for One No-Trump. With two four-card suits you should start with the lower, Respond Two Clubs, leaving partner room to bid diamonds next time if he has four.

(C) ♠ 65　　　　(D) ♠ K43
　　 ♡ 6　　　　　 ♡ 983
　　 ◇ AK754　　　 ◇ AQ65
　　 ♣ AJ865　　　 ♣ AJ6

With two five-card suits, as on Hand (C), both of which you intend to bid, it is best to start with the higher and bid your second suit on the next round. Bid Two Diamonds.

When you bid Three Clubs on the next round partner can easily show you delayed diamond support if he wants to, or else describe his hand in any other appropriate manner.

In the last lesson we told you what to bid with Hand (D) – Three No-Trumps, showing 13–15 HCP in a balanced hand with three-card support for hearts.

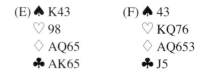

(E) ♠ K43　　　　(F) ♠ 43
　　 ♡ 98　　　　　 ♡ KQ76
　　 ◇ AQ65　　　　 ◇ AQ653
　　 ♣ AK65　　　　 ♣ J5

Hand (E) is too strong for Three No-Trumps and has insufficient heart support. But there is no need to panic. If you respond in a new suit, it is *forcing*. Partner will not pass and you can hear more about his hand before deciding on the final contract. Bid Two Clubs.

On Hand (F) you should raise partner immediately with your good support. You have enough for game so go straight to Four Hearts.

Lesson 41
More on responding in a suit

So far, all the responses in a suit to a one-level opening have been fairly straightforward. You have simply bid your longest suit at the lowest level (and we established what to do when you had two 'longest suits').

Sometimes it is more complicated. Your first question should be: 'Is my responding hand worth one or two bids?' With fewer than 11 HCP, game is unlikely if opener is minimum and your hand is worth only one bid. With 11 or more HCP, even if partner makes a minimum rebid, you will want to make a second response which invites him to consider a game contract.

Consider the following two hands after partner has opened One Heart:

(A)♠ KJ73
♡ 87
◇ AJ63
♣ 764

(B)♠ KJ73
♡ 87
◇ AJ63
♣ Q64

On both hands you respond One Spade. But with Hand (A) if partner rebids Two Hearts you will pass. If partner rebids Two Clubs you will give simple preference to Two Hearts (more on this later). As you will see in Lesson 44, a simple rebid in his own suit by opener shows a minimum hand. However, Hand (B) is stronger. Now you are worth a game invitation. If he rebids Two Hearts or Two Clubs you are worth Two No-Trumps. This shows similar values to an immediate

Two No-Trump response but you showed your four-card spade suit first.

If your hand is worth only one bid then priority must be given to showing major suits.

Consider these hands after partner has opened One Heart:

(C)♠ KJ43
♡ 87
◇ Q10765
♣ 76

(D)♠ KJ43
♡ K8
◇ Q10765
♣ 76

Hand (C) does not have the 9 HCP necessary for a two-level response, so you must respond One Spade. Although Hand (D) has 9 HCP it doesn't have the 11 necessary to intend to make two bids, so again it is better to show the major suit. Respond One Spade.

(E)♠ KJ43
♡ K8
◇ KQ10765
♣ 65

(F)♠ AQ54
♡ 6
◇ AKJ873
♣ K5

With Hand (E) you have enough to invite game facing a minimum rebid from partner. So there is no reason not to bid your longest suit first. Respond Two Diamonds, intending to bid Two Spades if partner rebids Two Hearts. Hand (F) is very strong, with possible slam prospects. Again, start by bidding your longest suit.

Lesson 42
Responding round-up

We have now covered all the basic responses to opening bids at the one level, so here is a quiz to test your understanding.

What would you respond to your partner's One Heart opening on the following hands?

(A) ♠ KJ105
    ♡ 5432
    ◇ AQ5
    ♣ 76

(B) ♠ KQ43
    ♡ 43
    ◇ QJ1072
    ♣ 76

(C) ♠ KJ1065
    ♡ 98
    ◇ AK1065
    ♣ 3

(D) ♠ Q4
    ♡ K43
    ◇ J1076
    ♣ Q1065

(E) ♠ K103
    ♡ KJ2
    ◇ KJ107
    ♣ K87

(F) ♠ 6543
    ♡ 9
    ◇ AKQ876
    ♣ 43

With Hand (A) raise to Three Hearts. You have found an eight-card fit so there is no need to bid your spades. On Hand (B) you don't have enough to bid at the two level so start with One Spade. Hand (C) is not a trick question. Just start with One Spade. On Hand (D), with 8 HCP, you don't have enough to bid at the two level but you can't support partner with only three cards, so start with One No-Trump. Hand (E) is perfect for an immediate jump to Three No-Trumps. On Hand (F) bid Two Diamonds and then rebid Three Diamonds if partner bid Two Hearts. Sometimes you might miss a 4-4 spade fit but it goes against the grain not to bid such a good diamond suit at all.

There is a refinement we have not yet covered. What would you respond to your partner's One Club opening?

(G) ♠ Q43
    ♡ K43
    ◇ J1076
    ♣ 763

(H) ♠ Q43
    ♡ K43
    ◇ KJ107
    ♣ 763

There is a convention that a One No-Trump response to a One Club opening shows 8–10 HCP, slightly more than over other openings. If you have 6–7 HCP, there is always an alternative. If you had a four-card suit other than clubs you could bid it, whereas if you had four clubs you could raise partner's suit. So with Hand (G) respond One Diamond, and with Hand (H) respond One No-Trump (it is better to make a descriptive limit bid if you can).

Lesson 43
Putting it into practice

Enough of all that bidding theory. It is time for a full hand to see how it works in practice. Deal out the hand for yourself and play it through until you are sure you understand everything that went on.

You pick up as South:

♠	KQ10743
♡	A72
◇	A5
♣	87

You have 13 HCP and, because you have two doubletons, an unbalanced hand. So you open with your longest suit, One Spade. Your partner, North, bids Two Clubs and East passes. What do you call?

You have a minimum opening bid, and have no second suit to bid, so you rebid your longest suit, Two Spades (see Lesson 44).

West passes, your partner raises to Three Spades and East passes. What do you call?

You have already described your hand as minimum but you do have a little extra. You could have had 12 HCP and you have 13. Also, you have a good, strong suit and two aces, which are always better than kings and queens. So you go on to Four Spades and this is the full hand:

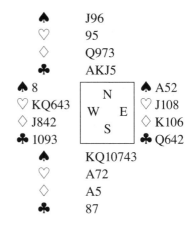

Contract: Four Spades by South
Lead: king of hearts

Count your tricks. You have five spades, one heart, one diamond (maybe two if West has the king) and two clubs (maybe three if West has the queen). You need one more trick.

Should you win the ace of hearts and draw trumps? No. If you do that you will need an extra trick in a minor suit. There is a better play than that.

Win the ace of hearts and return a low heart. West will win and the best he can do is to play a trump to East's ace and East plays a second trump. You win in hand and ruff your small heart in the dummy. Come back to your hand with the ace of diamonds and draw the last trump, making ten tricks in all.

Lesson 44
Rebids on minimum hands

If you have a minimum (12–14 HCP) balanced hand (remember: *no void, no singleton and not more than one doubleton*) you open One No-Trump. Whether you actually make a rebid or not depends upon partner's first response.

However, when you open One of a Suit and your partner replies in a different suit, *you promise a further bid*. Initially, he will assume your hand is unbalanced, but if you rebid in no-trumps he will adjust his thinking.

It is vital to recognise that when the opening bid is One of a Suit the bidding dialogue works progressively:

Opening bid: One Heart (I have at least four hearts and enough HCP to open the bidding).
First response: One Spade (I have at least four spades and 6+ HCP).
Rebid: Two Diamonds (my hand is unbalanced, at least five hearts and four diamonds, I have less than 19 HCP or I would have jumped to Three Diamonds).
Second response: Four Hearts (my three-card heart suit fits well with your five, and I have 12 HCP so I feel we should be in game).

This typical dialogue demonstrates how the opening One of a Suit and the first response of a simple change of suit quantify neither the shape nor HCP of either hand, but the rebid and second response set boundaries for both the shape and value of the joint holdings.

Here are some examples. You open One Heart and partner responds One Spade; what do you rebid?

(A) ♠ 65
♡ AQ7653
♢ A43
♣ Q6

(B) ♠ K764
♡ AJ765
♢ A5
♣ 74

With Hand (A) rebid your main suit, Two Hearts. With Hand (B) partner will be pleased to hear about your good support – rebid Two Spades. Both these rebids are *limit bids* and tell your partner immediately that you have a minimum hand.

(C) ♠ A3
♡ AQ654
♢ 87
♣ K1076

(D) ♠ Q4
♡ KJ542
♢ A102
♣ K92

With Hand (C) you rebid your second suit – Two Clubs. This is not a limit bid as you could have up to about 18 HCP. Two Clubs is not forcing, but partner should not pass unless he has a very poor hand. With Hand (D) you are in a fix. To rebid One No-Trump would show 15–17 HCP. But to rebid Two Hearts on a hand which is basically balanced also gives a poor picture of your hand. So, what has gone wrong? Your opening bid: it should have been One No-Trump.

Lesson 45
Rebids with extra values

Now we are going to look at stronger hands.

When partner responds at the one level

What would you rebid with the following hands after you opened One Heart and your partner responded One Spade?

(A) ♠ 6	(B) ♠ AK4
♡ KQJ1065	♡ AKJ1054
◇ AQ4	◇ 5
♣ AJ3	♣ J102

On Hands (A) and (B) you have a good six-card suit and at least an ace more than you needed for your opening bid, too much for a simple rebid. The solution is to make a jump rebid in your first suit, Three Hearts. Don't be tempted to raise spades on Hand (B) because your partner may have only a four-card suit.

(C) ♠ AQ5	(D) ♠ AQ5
♡ KJ105	♡ AKJ104
◇ AQ3	◇ K3
♣ Q107	♣ J43

Hands (C) and (D) are both balanced with 18 HCP. A One No-Trump rebid would show 15–17 HCP, so you must jump to Two No-Trumps to show 18–19. Although Hand (C) is perfectly balanced, Hand (D) is also very suitable for this rebid. Don't worry about the strong five-card heart suit or the lack of a stopper in clubs.

Both Three Hearts and Two No-Trumps are *limit* bids. They show extra values but are not forcing; partner may pass.

When partner responds at the two level

Is the situation different after a two-level response? Suppose you hold the following hands after opening One Heart and hearing a Two Diamond response from your partner:

(E) ♠ A4	(F) ♠ KJ3
♡ AKJ1065	♡ AQ103
◇ Q65	◇ K103
♣ K5	♣ A43

On Hand (E), with 17 HCP and a very strong six-card suit, rebid Three Hearts. On Hand (F), rebid Two No-Trumps showing 15–17.

The difference with these rebids over a two-level response is that they are *forcing*. The combination of an opening hand with extra values and a hand strong enough to respond at the two level adds up to a sequence where you should not stay out of game. Even a simple Two No-Trump rebid as on Hand (F) is forcing. Even if both hands were minimum (15+9) you would have 24 HCP between you, just one short of what you usually like for game.

Lesson 46
More bids with extra values

What would you rebid on the following hands after you opened One Heart and partner responded One Spade?

(A) ♠ AK65　　(B) ♠ 6
　　♡ A10652　　　♡ AKJ106
　　♢ KJ3　　　　　♢ AK1065
　　♣ 6　　　　　　♣ A4

With Hand (A) you have a fine hand in support of spades. You have 15 HCP and a singleton which may be worth something extra. Show partner this with a jump to Three Spades. Hand (B) is tremendously strong with 19 HCP and two five-card suits. Surely you must have a good chance of game even if partner has very little. Rather than make a simple Two Diamond rebid which would not be forcing, jump to Three Diamonds. A jump in a new suit is played as forcing to game so partner won't pass and you can investigate your best contract.

(C) ♠ KJ5　　(D) ♠ AK65
　　♡ AQ1054　　　♡ A10652
　　♢ AQJ5　　　　♢ AK3
　　♣ 5　　　　　　♣ 6

Hand (C) is tricky. Although you have significant extra values you cannot bid Three Diamonds because you are not strong enough to force to game facing a minimum partner. Bid a simple Two Diamonds. If

partner bids again you will show your extra strength and spade support.

Hand (D) is nearly an ace stronger than Hand (A) above. Don't give partner the opportunity to pass Three Spades, bid Four Spades yourself.

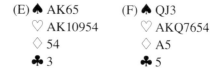

(E) ♠ AK65　　(F) ♠ QJ3
　　♡ AK10954　　　♡ AKQ7654
　　♢ 54　　　　　　♢ A5
　　♣ 3　　　　　　♣ 5

Hands (E) and (F) are examples of a very important principle of bidding unbalanced hands: distribution is more important than high-card points. With Hand (E), although you have only 14 HCP, partner needs as little as QJxx in spades for Four Spades to be a good contract, so bid it directly. Again, do not give him the chance to stop short of game. Hand (F) is also very powerful and has been improved by partner's One Spade bid. Four Hearts will be a reasonable contract if he has as little as the king of spades and only a singleton heart. Again, do not give him the chance to stop short of game – bid it yourself. When you get to Part V you will discover that you could have made a stronger bid in the first place.

Lesson 47
Putting it into practice

You pick up the following hand as South:

♠ Q1092
♡ KQ103
◇ AK4
♣ Q3

With four cards in each major you make your correct opening of One Heart. Your partner responds Two Clubs. What now?

Rebid Two No-Trumps, showing a balanced 15–17. Partner bids Three Hearts.

Your partner's Three Heart bid shows *three*-card support (with four-card support he would have raised hearts immediately). He wants you to bid Four Hearts if you have a five-card suit. As it is you bid Three No-Trumps, closing the auction.

West leads the queen of diamonds and this is what you can see:

	♠	J4
	♡	AJ2
	◇	652
	♣	A10765

♠ A83	N	♠ K765
♡ 874	W E	♡ 965
◇ QJ1093	S	◇ 87
♣ K2		♣ J984

	♠	Q1092
	♡	KQ103
	◇	AK4
	♣	Q3

South	West	North	East
1♡	Pass	2♣	Pass
2NT	Pass	3♡	Pass
3NT	All Pass		

Contract: Three No-Trumps by South
Lead: queen of diamonds

Start by counting your tricks. You have two spades once you have knocked out the ace and king, four hearts, two diamonds and one club (with good extra chances in the suit), making nine in all. Can you see any problems?

If the opposing diamonds are divided 5-2, the defenders are threatening to take three diamond tricks to go with the ace and king of spades. If you win with the king of diamonds and play a spade, one of the defenders will win and clear the diamonds; now when you lose to the other spade honour that defender may have three more diamonds to cash.

If the hand with the long diamonds has no spade honour there is no problem, and if he has both honours you cannot succeed. However, when the spade honours are in different defending hands (about 50% of the time) you can be sure of success. You must *duck the opening lead*. West will continue diamonds but now when East gets the lead with his king of spades he has no diamond to return so the suit cannot be established. You can knock out West's ace of spades with no damaging consequences.

Lesson 48
Reverses

Look at the following hands that we have seen before:

(A) ♠ A3
   ♡ AQ654
   ◇ 87
   ♣ K1076

(B) ♠ KJ5
   ♡ AQ1054
   ◇ AQJ5
   ♣ 5

In Lesson 44 we bid 1♡ – 1♠ – 2♣ with Hand (A). We commented at the time that while this bid was not *forcing*, it could be made on a very strong hand of, say, 18 HCP, so responder should strain to keep the bidding open if at all possible. Similarly, in Lesson 46 we bid 1♡ – 1♠ – 2◇ with Hand (B).

What these hands have in common is that their longest suit is higher-ranking than their second longest suit. Try these:

(C) ♠ A3
   ♡ 87
   ◇ K1076
   ♣ AQ654

(D) ♠ K1076
   ♡ 87
   ◇ A3
   ♣ AQ654

With Hand (C) you still open your longest suit, One Club, but you have a problem on the next round after partner responds, say, One Heart. You can't bid One No-Trump because that would show 15–17 HCP. If you were to rebid your second suit, diamonds, your poor partner, with a minimum hand that preferred clubs to diamonds would have to put you back to clubs at the three level. (On Hand (A),

when the bidding started 1♡ – 1♠ – 2♣, he could tell you that he preferred hearts without raising the level.) No, when you have a minimum hand (say 12–15) and you cannot rebid your second suit at the same level, you must simply rebid your first suit.

Hand (D) is the exception. Even though your second suit is higher ranking than your first, because you can bid it at the one level you should do so. This does not show extra values as your partner can still give you preference to your first suit at the two level.

The corollary to this is that when you do rebid a higher ranking suit you show extra values – about 16 or more HCP.

(F) ♠ KJ5
   ♡ AQJ5
   ◇ AQ1054
   ♣ 5

(G) ♠ 6
   ♡ AKJ106
   ◇ AK10652
   ♣ 4

So with both these hands you open One Diamond and rebid Two Hearts over partner's response of One Spade, One No-Trump or Two Clubs. This rebid is called a *reverse*. It is forcing for one round (or to game if the initial response was at the two level), guarantees at least five cards in the suit opened, and shows 16 or more HCP.

Try looking at it this way: if partner makes a rebid in a new suit that is at a level higher than Two of the suit he opened, then he is showing a strong hand.

Lesson 49
Responder's second bid 1

The principles governing responder's second bid are similar to those on the first round. We will first look at the situation where opener has shown a minimum hand. If responder has:

(a) a minimum hand (say 6–9 HCP), he should either pass or give simple preference to opener's first suit (i.e. put opener back to his first suit at the minimum level), or rebid his own suit, or bid One No-Trump
(b) something extra (10–12 HCP with a fit or 11–12 without a fit) he should make an invitational bid
(c) 13 HCP or more, he should make sure game is reached.

Here are some examples. Suppose the bidding has started 1♡ – 1♠ – 2♡:

(A)♠ KQ43	(B)♠ A98652
♡ 43	♡ 5
◇ QJ1072	◇ K54
♣ 76	♣ J54

Hand (A) is not that bad a hand but there is little prospect of game facing a minimum Two Heart rebid. Pass. On Hand (B) it may be tempting to bid Two Spades but how many hearts do you think partner has? Remember, he would open One No-Trump if he was balanced (no void, no singleton and no more than one doubleton), so his distribution

cannot be 5-3-3-2. If he is 5-4-2-2 he would bid his four-card suit in preference to rebidding his hearts, ergo he has a six-card suit. There is no reason to be afraid of a Two Heart contract. It is better to let things drop as quickly as possible. Pass.

(C)♠ KJ105	(D)♠ A10542
♡ 53	♡ K43
◇ AJ97	◇ A4
♣ Q109	♣ 1065

Both these 11-point hands are worth a game invitation. You have already shown your spade suit, so with Hand (C) bid Two No-Trumps and with Hand (D) bid Three Hearts.

(E)♠ QJ76	(F)♠ A10653
♡ 53	♡ A64
◇ AQ10	◇ KJ54
♣ A1042	♣ 3

Hands (E) and (F) are similar but a little stronger. Now you want to ensure that game is reached so bid Three No-Trumps and Four Hearts respectively.

These hands have been relatively straightforward because the right *denomination* has been fairly clear. This has meant that you could either bid game or make a sensible limit bid, depending on your values. It is not always as easy as that as you will see in the next lesson.

Lesson 50
Responder's second bid 2

Sometimes responder has sufficient values to make a second bid, maybe even to insist on game, but even after the first three bids of the auction the best trump suit is unclear. Look at the following hands after the auction 1♡ – 1♠ – 2♡:

(A)♠ KQJ105   (B)♠ AK7643
   ♡ 54   ♡ 5
   ◇ AK65   ◇ K762
   ♣ J6   ♣ 65

On Hand (A) perhaps you could jump straight to Four Hearts, since partner should have a six-card suit; but it seems a little premature with only a small doubleton in support. Either Four Spades or Three No-Trumps could be a better contract. There is no need for you to decide now. Bid Three Diamonds. A new suit bid by responder is always forcing (to game if that suit is bid at the three level). This gives partner the chance to bid his hearts yet again with a very strong suit, or give delayed support for your spades which he would do with, say, Ax. Alternatively he could bid Three No-Trumps if he had clubs well stopped.

In the last lesson we gave an example of a weaker hand than Hand (B) that had a six-card spade suit and a singleton heart. We said that the weaker hand should pass Two Hearts. This Hand (B) should bid Two Spades. This bid says, 'I know you have a six-card heart suit but I do not have a fit for you. However, I do have a six-card spade suit and a promising hand if you have a secondary fit for me.' Partner will usually pass but can bid on if his hand is suitable for playing in spades. Note that it would be wrong to bid Three Diamonds because the hand is not strong enough to force to game.

Although the hands we have looked at so far have been after the sequence 1♡ – 1♠ – 2♡, the principles are similar whatever the auction. After a sequence such as 1♡ – 1♠ – 2♠, responder's choices are to pass, invite game with Three Spades or go all the way to game himself.

Let us look at an auction such as 1♡ – 1♠ – 2♣. With a minimum (say, 5–8 HCP) hand responder can pass or give preference to Two Hearts; with invitational values responder usually chooses between Two No-Trumps, Three Clubs and Three Hearts; and with 13 HCP or more, responder bids game in what he thinks will be the best trump suit (or no-trumps).

Lesson 51
Responder's second bid 3

If opener makes a bid which shows extra values the principles governing responder's second bid are the same but it is often difficult for inexperienced players to appreciate that when opener shows a good hand they do not need such a great hand themselves in order to bid on.

Look at this ordinary responding hand:

♠	A1065
♡	1054
◇	Q5
♣	K1086

Now consider the following sequences:

(1)	**Opener**	**Resp'r**	(2)	**Opener**	**Resp'r**
	1◇	1♠		1◇	1♠
	2◇	?		3◇	?

On Sequence (1) responder has a clear pass, but on Sequence (2), where opener shows extra values and a six-card suit, he should try Three No-Trumps. The queen of diamonds should help solidify partner's suit and the ace of spades is a sure trick. All should be well if the opponents can't take too many hearts and there is no way to find that out. The game bonus is worth some risk. When your partnership's main suit is a minor but you have fairly balanced hands you should generally prefer to try Three No-Trumps because eleven tricks are a lot to make.

(3)	**Opener**	**Resp'r**	(4)	**Opener**	**Resp'r**
	1◇	1♠		1◇	1♠
	3♠	?		2NT	?

On Sequence (3), while responder would have happily passed a raise to Two Spades, it is clear to press on to game when partner shows extra values.

On Sequence (4) you are well worth a raise to Three No-Trumps, though you might have settled for a conservative raise to Two No-Trumps had partner simply rebid One No-Trump.

(5)	**Opener**	**Resp'r**	(6)	**Opener**	**Resp'r**
	1♡	1♠		1◇	1♠
	3◇	?		3♣	?

On Sequence (5) partner has forced to game (i.e. shown 19 HCP or equivalent) with at least five hearts and at least four diamonds. You should show your three-card support for his first suit by giving him preference to Three Hearts. On Sequence (6) partner has also forced to game but this time has five diamonds and four clubs. Although you have only 9 HCP you have a great hand – the queen of his first suit, four-card support headed by the king for his second suit and an ace on the side. Raise him to Four Clubs because there may be a slam in clubs – but more of this in a future lesson.

Lesson 52
Putting it into practice

As South you pick up the following cards:

♠	AQJ1074
♡	5
◇	KJ83
♣	107

North opens One Heart and rebids Two Hearts over your One Spade response. What now? Although you have a good hand, it is not quite worth forcing to game. To rebid Two Spades would carry some invitational overtones because there is no need to 'rescue' partner from his freely rebid Two Heart contract, but with a strong suit that needs no support, as here, jump to *Three* Spades, asking partner to bid Four with reasonable controls (aces and kings). Here partner bids Four Spades. West leads the ace and king of clubs and switches to a trump:

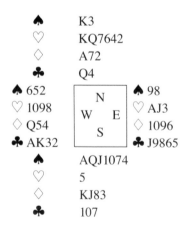

```
              ♠ K3
              ♡ KQ7642
              ◇ A72
              ♣ Q4
  ♠ 652              ♠ 98
  ♡ 1098      N      ♡ AJ3
  ◇ Q54    W     E   ◇ 1096
  ♣ AK32      S      ♣ J9865
              ♠ AQJ1074
              ♡ 5
              ◇ KJ83
              ♣ 107
```

Contract: Four Spades by South.
Lead: ace and king of clubs followed by a trump switch.

As usual, start by counting your tricks. You have six spades, one heart (once you have knocked out the ace) and two diamonds. You can always fall back on the diamond finesse for your tenth trick but can you see any other chances?

The answer lies in the heart suit. You will always be able to discard one diamond loser on a top heart once you have knocked out the ace but you may well be able to do better.

Win West's trump switch in hand and at trick four play a heart. If West has the ace you are in a very strong position. If he wins his ace, you now have two top hearts on which to discard both losing diamonds. A better play would be for him to withhold his ace so your king of hearts wins in dummy but now you have not lost a heart trick, so you can afford to lose a diamond trick.

Now suppose East has the ace of hearts, as here. He wins his ace and plays a second trump. You win in dummy and ruff a heart high. Now draw the outstanding trumps, cross to the ace of diamonds and test the hearts. If they have broken 3-3, your problems are over; if they are not good you can fall back on the diamond finesse for your contract.

Lesson 53
Bidding practice

We are coming to the end of the basic bidding section. In this lesson we will look at the bidding of two pairs of hands. Start by looking at just the hands and write down how you think the bidding should go before reading on. West is the dealer on both hands.

```
      ♠ Q3        ┌─────┐    ♠ AK764
      ♡ K54       │  N  │    ♡ AQ982
      ◇ KJ53    W │     │ E  ◇ 8
      ♣ KJ85      │  S  │    ♣ 96
                  └─────┘
```

West	East
1NT	3♠
3NT	4♡
Pass	

West opens One No-Trump with his balanced hand and 13 HCP. East has enough for game so must jump in one of his suits – it is normal to start with the higher ranking when bidding two five-card suits. West does not have support for spades so bids Three No-Trumps. East now knows that his partner must have at least three-card support for hearts (remember that part of the definition of a balanced hand was 'no more than one doubleton'), so bids Four Hearts, the final contract.

```
  ♠ 65          ┌─────┐    ♠ AQ732
  ♡ AQJ1083     │  N  │    ♡ K
  ◇ 32        W │     │ E  ◇ 985
  ♣ AJ3         │  S  │    ♣ KQ72
                └─────┘
```

West	East
1♡	1♠
2♡	3♣
3♡	4♡
Pass	

The first two bids are easy. Then West rebids his heart suit to show an unbalanced hand. East has enough points for game but does not yet know the best denomination so he bids his second suit, clubs. This new suit at the three level is forcing to game. It is up to West, now, to make the best descriptive bid he can. He can't bid no-trumps because he doesn't have a stopper in the unbid suit, diamonds, and he would need four-card support to raise clubs. His best solution is to bid his hearts yet again, telling partner that the suit is very strong. (If his hearts were less strong and he had, say, Kx in spades, he could *give preference* to Three Spades – this delayed support for partner only shows a doubleton.) This is what East wanted to hear: the singleton king of hearts is clearly enough support for West's strong suit so East bids Four Hearts.

Lesson 54
Putting it into practice

You pick up as South (with opponents silent throughout):

♠ KJ2
♡ J43
◇ Q109732
♣ 6

Your partner opens One Club, you respond One Diamond and he rebid One Heart. What do you bid now?

Your partner has shown five clubs and four hearts and although he has promised no extra values his top limit is about 18 HCP. You have a good spade stopper, so your most natural bid is One No-Trump – after all, Three No-Trumps is your most likely game.

Your partner raises you to Three No-Trumps. West leads the four of spades and this is what you can see:

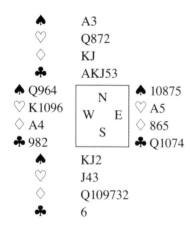

```
            ♠ A3
            ♡ Q872
            ◇ KJ
            ♣ AKJ53
♠ Q964      ┌──────┐   ♠ 10875
♡ K1096     │   N  │   ♡ A5
◇ A4        │ W   E│   ◇ 865
♣ 982       │   S  │   ♣ Q1074
            └──────┘
            ♠ KJ2
            ♡ J43
            ◇ Q109732
            ♣ 6
```

Contract: Three No-Trumps by South
Lead: four of spades

Start as usual by counting your tricks. The spade lead has given you three tricks in that suit; when you have knocked out the ace of diamonds you will have five there; and clubs should provide at least two. Can you see any problems?

If you run the opening lead round to your hand and play a diamond, the defenders might duck and only win the second round. Now you have communication problems. If the lay-out is as it is here, they will now be able to defeat you. West switches to a club instead of continuing spades. You cannot reach your hand and will eventually lose two clubs, two hearts and a diamond.

When you counted your tricks, you should have realised that the total came to ten and you needed only nine. Don't be greedy. Win the ace of spades in the dummy and play the king of diamonds. Now the defenders cannot deny you two spades, five diamonds and two clubs which add up to the nine you need.

Part III

Defence

Many beginners find defence boring. You can sometimes see them daydreaming, just waiting for the hand to be over so there is a new deal and they may get the chance to be declarer. This is a great pity and a great waste. You can expect to defend twice as often as you are declarer, so if you do not take an interest in this part of the game you will miss a lot of fun. Defence can be one of the most fascinating aspects of bridge but there are a few ground rules to learn.

Lesson 55
Opening leads 1

On average you will defend on half the deals; you will be declarer on only a quarter. If you are going to enjoy bridge to the full, it is vital that you take an interest in defence. If you and your partner can legitimately exchange information about each other's hand you will soon find it easier to defend accurately. It all starts with the opening lead.

We considered opening leads in some early MiniBridge lessons, where we had the advantage of seeing dummy before making the lead. In bridge proper we don't have this help, so we have to work out how much information is at our disposal to select the best possible opening lead for us in defence. You may find it helpful in developing this skill to discipline yourself to think: (1) which suit should I lead? then (2) which card from that suit?

Which suit?

If you hold AKQJx or KQJ10x of a suit, it is usually right to start off with it more or less whatever the sequence. You don't often hold such an obvious lead, however. More frequently you hold a motley collection of minor honours and need to choose a lead.

If partner has bid a suit, it is usually a good idea to lead it. Even if it turns out badly, it will keep him happy.

If no one has bid any suits (e.g. 1NT – 3NT), fourth highest of your longest and strongest is as good a rule as any (see Lesson 17). If it is a toss-up between a major and a minor, you should choose the major – after all, your opponents have not looked for a major-suit fit.

If the enemy has bid some suits, this can be a great help. You will be leading through dummy's cards to your partner, with declarer playing last. So, while it is often a good idea to lead dummy's suit (lead through strength), you want to avoid leading a suit declarer has bid. It often works well to lead declarer's shortest suit, particularly when you think partner has length and strength there.

South	West	North	East
1♡	Pass	1♠	Pass
2♡	Pass	3♣	Pass
3NT	All Pass		

You would certainly *not* lead hearts. Dummy is likely to have five spades and four clubs, making the latter more attractive most of the time. However, if you have, say, a small doubleton in spades, a lead of that suit (declarer's likely shortage) could work very well. Declarer will surely have a diamond stopper but will probably have fewer than four cards in the suit (he didn't rebid Two Diamonds over One Spade). Generally, choose a diamond or a club. Look at the texture of these suits in your hand and make your final decision.

Lesson 56
Opening leads 2

Once you have chosen which suit to lead, you still have to decide which card to lead from that suit.

A lead from a suit headed by one honour (not the ace)

Against a suit contract or no-trumps, lead your fourth highest (see Lesson 17). From the following holdings lead the four:

(A)   K9743   (B)   Q954

From three to an honour you should choose your lowest card (against no-trumps you would not normally choose to lead from a three-card suit unless partner had bid it). Note that in this context the ten also counts as an honour.

A lead from a suit headed by the ace

You would also lead fourth highest against a no-trump contract, but it is inadvisable to lead low from an ace against a suit contract – if declarer or dummy has a singleton you may never make your ace. Indeed, unless you have a strong reason for choosing this suit it is better to choose another suit altogether.

A lead from a suit without an honour

Here, against both a suit contract and no-trumps, the common practice is to lead your second highest card from a three-, four- or five-card holding.

With a three-card suit you play your highest card next. This is known as MUD (Middle Up Down). With a four- or five-card suit, play your original fourth-best next.

If you started with a doubleton, then lead your top card on the first round.

A lead from a suit with two or more honours

If you have three honours in a suit you should always lead one of them (against a suit or no-trumps): top of touching honours.

(D)   KQJ65   (E)   KQ1065

(F)   KJ1065   (G)   Q1093

From (D) and (E) lead the king. From (F) and (G), where the honour sequence is broken, lead the top of the touching honours, the jack on (F) and the ten on (G).

With only two non-touching honours, just lead your fourth highest (e.g. lead the four from KJ64).

With two touching honours against a suit contract, lead the higher honour, but against a no-trump contract lead your fourth highest.

It is important to follow these guidelines because much defensive thinking is based on information given by the opening lead.

Lesson 57
Third hand play

Here we will consider the play to trick one by the partner of the opening leader.

Look at the following situations when partner leads a low card, promising an honour in the suit:

```
              985
2 led       [        ]    A76
```

When declarer plays low from dummy, you should win your ace. Most people find this quite easy – it is second nature to try to win tricks. This is harder:

```
              985
2 led       [        ]    K76
```

It is surprising how many people don't like to play their king. They are afraid it will be 'wasted'. True, it may not win the trick, but it will help 'build' a trick in partner's hand. Suppose the lay-out is:

```
                985
Q1042       [        ]    K76
                AJ3
```

If you play low declarer will win his jack, but if you play the king declarer will have to win the ace and now partner's Q10, sitting over declarer's jack, will make two tricks.

So far, it has been right to play your honour because you knew partner also had an honour. The situation is different if partner leads a high spot card, denying an honour:

```
              762
9 led       [        ]    K10543
```

Perhaps partner has led the suit because you bid it. You know he won't have an honour. Declarer has AQJ, or maybe AQJ8. Your king is doomed whatever you do but if you play your king at trick one declarer won't need to use up one of his entries to dummy to take another finesse. Part of a defender's task is to make life harder for declarer, so play a low card, not your king.

If partner leads an honour and you hold the honour immediately above it, you should normally play your highest spot card to encourage him to continue the suit.

```
              762
Q led       [        ]    K84
```

Play the eight, encouraging partner to continue.

If your honour is a doubleton however, you should play it in order to avoid blocking the suit:

```
              762
Q led       [        ]    K4
```

Play the king. This takes courage.

Lesson 58
Play with touching honours

In Lesson 56 we said that when you were on lead against a suit contract with two (or more) touching honours you should lead the top of the sequence. There is a good reason for this. Consider the following lay-out (against a suit contract):

```
              765
Q led     [        ]     A832
```

Suppose that your style was to lead honours randomly; sometimes you led the queen from queen-jack and sometimes from king-queen. Would you like your partner to play the ace at trick one and find that the lay-out was:

```
              765
KQ4       [        ]     A832
              J109
```

Or should he play small and find the suit distributed:

```
              765
QJ1094    [        ]     A832
               K
```

Defence is harder than declarer play because the defending side can see only half of its side's assets. To defend accurately you need to be able to build up a clear picture of the whole hand and you can do so only if your partner gives you helpful information.

Now look at the situation from the other side of the table:

```
              985
2 led     [        ]     QJ6
```

Do you play the queen or the jack to the first trick? The answer is to play the jack, the lower of touching honours. Suppose the lay-out is:

```
              985
K1042     [        ]     QJ6
              A73
```

When declarer wins your jack with his ace, your partner will know that you hold the queen, for if declarer held the ace and queen he would have won with the queen. If you were to play the queen, partner would not know who had the jack.

This is not to be confused with the opening lead where you lead the top of touching honours. If you are the first player in your partnership to play to a trick you play the top of touching honours; if your partner has already played to the trick you play the lowest.

Lesson 59
More on third hand play

We have now covered the basics of the opening lead and what the leader's partner should play at trick one when there are small cards in the dummy. When there are honour cards in the dummy the situation is slightly different. Let's look at some lay-outs:

```
                Q76
2 led        [        ]   KJ5
```

Here, assuming declarer plays low from dummy, it would be silly to play your king. If partner has the ace your jack will win the trick; then you can cash your king and play to partner's ace. If declarer has the ace, your jack will force it out and your king can make a trick on the next round. In each case declarer will make an extra trick if you play your king on the first round. If you have the two honours 'surrounding' dummy's honour, you should always play your lower honour if declarer plays low from dummy.

Sometimes you have to make a choice

Now suppose you hold K105 instead of KJ5. Your partner leads a low card, promising either the ace, the jack or both. These are the possible lay-outs:

```
                Q76
AJ42        [        ]   K105
                983
```

If you play the ten it will hold the trick. Then you cash the king and partner's ace. If you played the king at trick one dummy's queen would win the third round.

```
                Q76
J942        [        ]   K105
                A83
```

If you play the ten it will force declarer's ace. When partner next gains the lead he can play the jack and you will win dummy's queen with your king. Partner will also make his nine. If you play the king at trick one declarer will win his ace and later the queen, making an extra trick.

```
                Q76
A942        [        ]   K105
                J83
```

This time it does not matter. If you play the ten declarer will win the jack and you can later cash the king and ace. Alternatively you can cash the king and ace straight away.

So, on two lay-outs it gains to play your ten and on the third it doesn't make any difference. Quite a strong argument for playing the ten.

The same is true when you hold AJx over dummy's Kxx. Deal out all the possible combinations for yourself until you are sure you understand.

Lesson 60
Putting it all into practice

Enough of all this theory. Time for a hand.

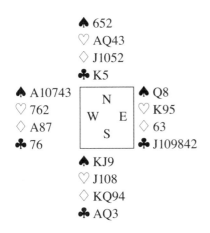

♠ 652
♡ AQ43
◇ J1052
♣ K5

♠ A10743   ♠ Q8
♡ 762   N   ♡ K95
◇ A87   W   E   ◇ 63
♣ 76   S   ♣ J109842

♠ KJ9
♡ J108
◇ KQ94
♣ AQ3

South	West	North	East
1◇	Pass	1♡	Pass
1NT	Pass	3NT	All Pass

South's bidding shows a hand with 15–17 HCP and at least four diamonds. It also denies four spades (he would have either opened One Spade or rebid One Spade on the second round) or four hearts (he would have raised North's suit).

As West you lead the four of spades. Partner plays the queen and declarer the king. Declarer now plays the king of diamonds from hand which you win with the ace. Who has the jack of spades? If partner has it you should continue with a low card in the suit, but if declarer has it you need to switch.

It is not a guess. Declarer has the jack of spades. If partner had held it he would have played it at trick one. You must switch. There is no clear indication which suit to play but on balance a heart is probably safer. On the actual lay-out declarer has no choice but to take the finesse and now your partner can play a second spade and you can cash four tricks in the suit.

On the actual deal declarer had no chance unless you had both the ace of diamonds and the king of hearts which was unlikely because you did not overcall One Spade. Can you see how he could have played the hand better so that he would have succeeded if your partner had had the ace of diamonds?

Deal out the hand for yourself but swap over the ace and six of diamonds. Now look at the effect of ducking the first round of spades entirely. East continues with the eight of spades to declarer's jack and whether West wins this spade or not the defence is doomed as East has no more spades to play when he gets in with the king of hearts.

A final note on the bidding. Although North has four-card support for his partner's diamonds it is right to start by introducing his heart suit, looking for a 4-4 fit. When South rebids One No-Trump, showing 15–17 HCP, there is still no reason for North to show the diamond support. He has a balanced hand too and should simply raise to Three No-Trumps.

Lesson 61
Basic signals

If the defenders are to build up an accurate picture of the concealed hands it is important that they use all the legitimate methods at their disposal. We should point out here that any physical expressions of pleasure or displeasure about partner's defence (e.g. smiles, frowns, squirms, tut-tuts etc) are illegitimate signals and thoroughly disapproved of in most circles.

Signalling and discarding well with your partner takes much practice, so don't expect always to get it right.

Signalling on partner's lead

The main thing partner usually wants to know is whether or not you like his lead. If you like it you play a high card; if you don't like it you play a low card. This is called an *attitude* signal. If it is completely obvious what your honour holding is in the suit, then you should tell partner how many cards you hold in the suit. This is called a *count* signal.

A43

K led [   ]   72

Partner has presumably led from KQx(x). Play the two, an attitude signal, to tell him that you don't hold the jack.

AJ3

K led [   ]   72

Now he knows you don't have an honour. Play the seven, a count signal, telling him you have an even number of cards in the suit.

Signalling on declarer's lead

Here is it easier to work out the honour location from the way declarer plays a suit. The most important thing to tell your partner is how many cards you have in the suit. Play your second highest (as long as you don't think you will need it for trick-taking purposes) from four, the lowest from three and the highest from two.

Signalling when giving a ruff

When you know (or hope) that partner has no cards left in a suit and you are leading it for him to ruff you can help him know what to play next by choosing carefully which card you play. If you play a low card you are asking him to play the lower of the two remaining suits (not trumps nor, obviously, the suit he is ruffing), while if you play a high card you are asking for the higher suit. This is known as a *suit-preference* signal.

Discarding

When you can't follow suit, then you should discard low cards in suits you don't want partner to play or high cards in suits that you would like him to play.

Lesson 62
Do you like the lead?

Here is another complete deal to study:

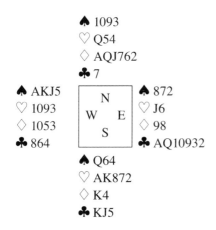

```
                  ♠ 1093
                  ♡ Q54
                  ◇ AQJ762
                  ♣ 7
    ♠ AKJ5      ┌─────────┐    ♠ 872
    ♡ 1093      │    N    │    ♡ J6
    ◇ 1053      │  W   E  │    ◇ 98
    ♣ 864       │    S    │    ♣ AQ10932
                └─────────┘
                  ♠ Q64
                  ♡ AK872
                  ◇ K4
                  ♣ KJ5
```

South	West	North	East
1♡	Pass	2◇	Pass
2NT	Pass	3♡	Pass
4♡	All Pass		

Contract: Four Hearts by South
Lead: ace of spades

South's bidding shows 15–17 HCP and a five-card heart suit. With only four hearts he would have rebid Three No-Trumps after his partner showed three-card heart support with his Three Heart bid.

You lead the ace of spades and your partner plays the two. What do you next?

Dummy is very strong for his bidding. There are two possible ways you might defeat Four Hearts:

(1) If partner has Qxx in spades you could take three rounds of the suit and hope to come to one more trick in the outside suits. As declarer has at least 15 HCP (he rebid Two No-Trumps) your partner has at most 8 HCP (you can see 17 HCP between your hand and dummy). There is room for partner to hold the ace of hearts, king of diamonds or ace of clubs.

(2) If partner has just three small spades you need to find him with an entry. Then you can put him in and a lead through declarer's queen will allow you to take three spade tricks in total to go with the outside trick.

It is important you do the right thing. If you switch and partner has the queen of spades declarer may have the ace and king of clubs and be able to discard one of dummy's spades before losing whatever trick he must lose in the red suits. If you continue spades and declarer has the queen you will have given him a gratuitous trick.

The key is in partner's play to trick one. He played the two of spades, discouraging you from playing another spade. You must play him for an outside entry and the most likely place for him to hold it is in clubs. Switch to the six of clubs and let him play another spade through declarer's queen.

Lesson 63
Can partner ruff?

Are these practice deals persuading you that defence can be interesting after all?

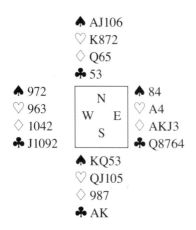

```
              ♠ AJ106
              ♡ K872
              ◇ Q65
              ♣ 53
  ♠ 972      ┌──────┐      ♠ 84
  ♡ 963      │  N   │      ♡ A4
  ◇ 1042     │ W  E │      ◇ AKJ3
  ♣ J1092    │  S   │      ♣ Q8764
             └──────┘
              ♠ KQ53
              ♡ QJ105
              ◇ 987
              ♣ AK
```

South	West	North	East
1♡	Pass	3♡	Pass
4♡	All Pass		

Contract: Four Hearts by South
Lead: jack of clubs

When West leads the jack of clubs against Four Hearts, as East you should play the four to discourage (after all, if partner were to be on lead again you would like him to play a diamond, not a club). Declarer wins the king and plays the queen of hearts to your ace. What do you do now?

You should play the king of diamonds. When declarer plays low on this trick, partner will know for certain that you hold the ace. Therefore you cannot possibly want to know about his honours in the suit, so he will tell you how many diamonds he holds. He plays the two. What now?

He has shown you an odd number of diamonds, hopefully three – if declarer has a singleton he will surely make his contract. So now you know that if you cash the ace of diamonds you will set up dummy's queen; if partner has no other trick Four Hearts will make. Your only chance is to get off lead as safely as you can and hope that you have to come to two more diamond tricks at the end.

Play another club and sit back and hope. If the lay-out is as above, and declarer has the same distribution as dummy, then this passive defence will beat the game.

Had partner played a high diamond under your king you would have known he had an even number of cards in the suit. Your best chance now of defeating the game would be to find partner with a doubleton diamond. If it turns out that he had four and that your play in the suit established dummy's queen, it is unlikely that you could have beaten the contract whatever you had done.

Lesson 64
A switch in time

Here is a hand for you to defend which will bring out some aspects of what you have learned over the past few lessons. Don't forget to get a pack of cards and set it out.

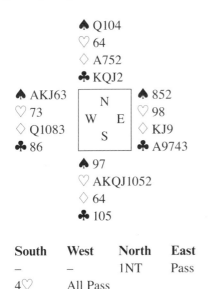

♠ Q104
♡ 64
◇ A752
♣ KQJ2

♠ AKJ63
♡ 73
◇ Q1083
♣ 86

♠ 852
♡ 98
◇ KJ9
♣ A9743

♠ 97
♡ AKQJ1052
◇ 64
♣ 105

South	West	North	East
–	–	1NT	Pass
4♡	All Pass		

Contract: Four Hearts by South
Lead: ace of spades

You have an easy choice of lead against South's Four Hearts: the ace of spades. With the queen in dummy, partner knows that you know that he has no honour, for you would have had no reason to lead an unsupported ace. So he plays the two to show you an odd number. While it is possible this is a singleton, it is much more likely that it is declarer, with his long heart suit, who is short in spades. If declarer has a doubleton spade you can see that if you cash the king you will set up dummy's queen for a discard.

So you must switch, hoping to set up a trick to cash when you get in with your king of spades. The club suit doesn't seem to offer much prospect but there is just room for partner to have the ace of clubs and the king of diamonds.

So, at trick two you switch to the three of diamonds. Declarer wins with the ace, draws trumps in two rounds and plays the ten of clubs. You play the eight, to show your doubleton. This cannot be from a three-card suit so declarer cannot have a singleton and it is safe for your partner to duck his ace of clubs. Declarer continues with a second club. Your partner wins his ace and plays the king and jack of diamonds. Declarer ruffs but cannot get to dummy for his established clubs so you must make your king of spades at the end.

Note that your careful signalling and partner's subsequent duck in the club suit meant you could afford to make a mistake in cashing your winners at the end. If East had won the first club and then tried to cash two diamonds he would have let declarer make his contract.

Lesson 65
Suit-preference signal

When giving partner a ruff, it is important to help him decide what to play next. Cover up the West and South hands before reading on.

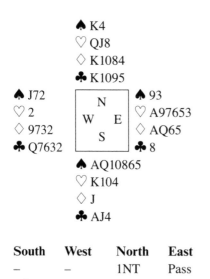

```
              ♠ K4
              ♡ QJ8
              ◇ K1084
              ♣ K1095
♠ J72      ┌─────────┐    ♠ 93
♡ 2        │    N    │    ♡ A97653
◇ 9732     │  W   E  │    ◇ AQ65
♣ Q7632    │    S    │    ♣ 8
           └─────────┘
              ♠ AQ10865
              ♡ K104
              ◇ J
              ♣ AJ4
```

South	West	North	East
–	–	1NT	Pass
4♠	All Pass		

Contract: Four Spades by South
Lead: two of hearts

Your partner leads the two of hearts against Four Spades. You win the ace as declarer plays the four. How do you plan to beat the contract?

Your best hope seems to be to find partner with a singleton heart. Then all you need to do is give him a ruff, he can put you in with the ace of diamonds and you can give him another ruff. With any luck you may make another diamond trick and beat the contract by two tricks. Can you see any problems?

Although you can see exactly how to beat Four Spades, it may not be so easy for your partner. How is he to know whether you have the ace of diamonds or the ace of clubs? This is where suit-preference signals come in very useful. The heart you play to give him his ruff should help him find your outside entry.

Lead the nine of hearts, your highest card in the suit. After partner has ruffed he should play a diamond (the highest-ranking non-trump suit) to dummy's king and your ace. Now play the seven of hearts to give partner his second ruff. After all, you would like him to play another diamond, just in case you can beat the contract by two. As it happens declarer ruffs the diamond and you will have to settle for one down.

Can you see what declarer might have done to make it harder for you? He should have dropped the king of hearts under your ace at trick one. Now, if you were persuaded that your partner had led from 1042, playing another heart would have risked giving declarer two quick discards. You might well have preferred to play partner for the ace of clubs and switched to that suit. After all, declarer need not have had such a good hand for his jump to Four Spades.

Lesson 66
Should you encourage?

One thing you must always remember when you are defending is your *target*. Even if you have a useful holding in the suit partner has led, you may need to look elsewhere for enough tricks to beat the contract. Cover up the West and South hands before reading on.

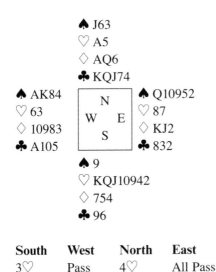

♠ J63
♥ A5
♦ AQ6
♣ KQJ74

♠ AK84
♥ 63
♦ 10983
♣ A105

♠ Q10952
♥ 87
♦ KJ2
♣ 832

♠ 9
♥ KQJ10942
♦ 754
♣ 96

South	West	North	East
3♥	Pass	4♥	All Pass

Contract: Four Hearts by South
Lead: ace of spades

South's opening bid of Three Hearts is something we have not yet covered but we will do so later (see Lesson 143). It shows a weak hand in high-card points but a good long suit, usually a seven-carder.

West leads the ace of spades and you must decide whether to play the ten or the two. (It

would be a mistake to play any other card – if you are going to signal you should make it as clear as possible to partner.)

Perhaps you think that you should encourage because you have the queen. Is this not the same situation as in Lesson 62?

No, it is not the same situation. Here you know it is unlikely that you can beat the contract in the spade suit. Indeed, you may be able to take only one spade.

What you can see is lots of club tricks in dummy. Once partner's ace is knocked out that suit will provide several tricks for declarer. Partner must switch to a diamond.

You should discourage spades by playing the two. Now partner should switch to the ten of diamonds. Declarer will finesse as it is the only chance for his contract. You will take your king and return the jack of diamonds. Declarer's best play is to win and play a club immediately but your partner will win and cash a diamond to beat Four Hearts.

Perhaps you are wondering how partner knew to cash a diamond trick and not a spade. It was because you continued with the *jack* of diamonds after winning your king. Just as with the opening lead, there is a convention that when returning partner's suit, you play your original fourth-highest. So, had you held ♠Q1052 and ♦KJ72, you would have returned the *two* of diamonds. Now your partner would have known to cash a spade when in with the ace of clubs.

Lesson 67
No time to waste

On this hand you need to hurry if you are going to beat declarer's contract. Cover up the West and South hands before reading on.

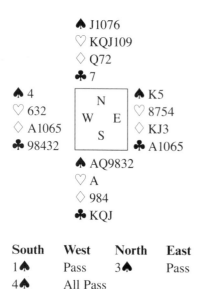

♠ J1076
♡ KQJ109
♢ Q72
♣ 7

♠ 4
♡ 632
♢ A1065
♣ 98432

♠ K5
♡ 8754
♢ KJ3
♣ A1065

♠ AQ9832
♡ A
♢ 984
♣ KQJ

South	West	North	East
1♠	Pass	3♠	Pass
4♠	All Pass		

Contract: Four Spades by South
Lead: eight of clubs

As East you win the ace of clubs and declarer drops the jack. Do you automatically lead back partner's suit or can you think of anything better to do?

It is clear that declarer has plenty of tricks. The spade finesse is right for him; he has four or five heart tricks; partner's lead and declarer's play at trick one suggest a couple of club winners as well. The only chance is to take some diamond tricks and the only time to do that is now.

It may seem dangerous to lead a diamond from the king. Indeed, if declarer has the ace he could make an extra trick by running the diamond round to dummy's queen. But in that case nothing can be done. Suppose instead you continue with a club. Declarer will ruff in dummy, draw trumps and play a heart. Partner will win his ace (if he doesn't have the ace of diamonds he probably has the ace of hearts), but that will be the last trick for the defence. The reality is that if declarer has the ace of diamonds the contract cannot be defeated; in fact it will probably make an overtrick.

Switch to a low diamond at trick two. If, as here, declarer has three small, you will beat the game.

One of the most important things to decide when defending is whether or not there is a need to hurry. Sometimes an active defence will merely help a declarer who would have struggled if left to his own devices; on the other hand there are other situations where it is vital to take tricks immediately.

Lesson 68
Rule of eleven

Usually, unless you have a particularly good suit of your own, it is a good idea to return the suit partner has led at trick one. However, sometimes you can work out that that suit can't be good enough to beat the contract. Cover up the West and South hands before reading on.

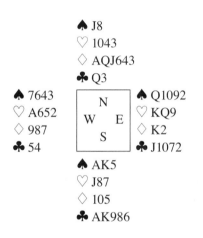

♠ J8
♡ 1043
◇ AQJ643
♣ Q3

♠ 7643　　♠ Q1092
♡ A652　　♡ KQ9
◇ 987　　　◇ K2
♣ 54　　　♣ J1072

♠ AK5
♡ J87
◇ 105
♣ AK986

South	West	North	East
1♣	Pass	1◇	Pass
1NT	Pass	3NT	All Pass

Contract: Three No-Trumps by South
Lead: six of spades

West leads the six of spades against South's Three No-Trumps. Declarer plays the jack from dummy and wins your queen with his king. He then runs the ten of diamonds which you win. What now?

Perhaps partner has led from Axxxx in spades and you can beat declarer by returning a spade. In Lesson 17 we discussed this type of situation. If partner has led a fourth-highest card you know he has three cards higher than the spot card he has led. Consider the six: in total there are eight cards higher. If partner has three there are five remaining in the other three hands. If you do a similar calculation for the other spot cards, you will find that if you deduct the value of the spot card led from eleven, you get the total number of cards higher than it in the other three hands. This is called the *Rule of Eleven* and it can be quite helpful.

Here it tells you that there are five cards higher than the six in the North, East and South hands. The trouble is that you have seen six of them! North had two, you had three and declarer has played one. The conclusion to be drawn is that partner's lead is second highest from some number of small cards, not fourth highest from an honour.

Declarer surely has nine tricks now diamonds are established. Your only chance is to take four tricks immediately and the only way to do that is to hope that partner has Axxx in hearts. Switch to the king of hearts, continuing when it holds with the queen and a third heart.

Lesson 69
Counting

The single most important thing to do when defending or declaring a hand is to count: count tricks, count points, count distribution. It doesn't sound very difficult; the most you need to count to is 40 (for points). The problem is getting into good habits and remembering to count.

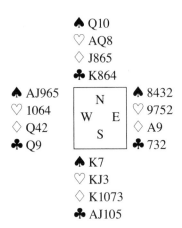

♠ Q10
♡ AQ8
◇ J865
♣ K864

♠ AJ965　♠ 8432
♡ 1064　♡ 9752
◇ Q42　◇ A9
♣ Q9　♣ 732

♠ K7
♡ KJ3
◇ K1073
♣ AJ105

South	West	North	East
–	–	1♣	Pass
1◇	1♠	2◇	2♠
3NT	All Pass		

Contract: Three No-Trumps by South
Lead: six of spades

North-South were playing the strong no-trump. In that system you open with a suit and rebid no-trumps to show 12–14 points.

West led the six of spades which declarer won with the queen in dummy. Since East's honour holding in spades was more or less known (he could not beat the queen) he could afford to show West how many he held by starting a *peter* (i.e. intending to play high-low to show an even number). Declarer decided to play for the drop in clubs and so cashed four tricks in that suit. She followed up by cashing three rounds of hearts. Meanwhile West had to find some discards. Without giving the matter much thought he decided that he ought to hold on to his diamond stopper. After all, he didn't want declarer dropping his queen in that suit as well. So West discarded a couple of spades. Now declarer played a diamond to the king for her contract.

West failed to count that nine tricks were certain if declarer held the ace of diamonds. The only hope was to play for partner to hold that card. East had played high-low in spades, so declarer was known to have a doubleton in the suit (simple counting again). If East had the ace of diamonds he would go in with it on the first round and play back a spade, enabling West to cash all his remaining winners in the suit to defeat the contract. Keeping the queen of diamonds protected was wrong.

Lesson 70
Deduction from the opening lead

Often the opening lead can tell you a great deal about the whole hand, not just about one suit. Look at what East was able to deduce from his partner's lead on this deal. Cover up the West and South hands before reading on.

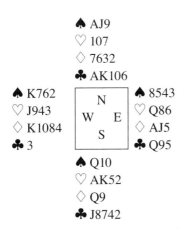

```
              ♠ AJ9
              ♡ 107
              ◇ 7632
              ♣ AK106
♠ K762      ┌───────┐   ♠ 8543
♡ J943      │   N   │   ♡ Q86
◇ K1084     │ W   E │   ◇ AJ5
♣ 3         │   S   │   ♣ Q95
            └───────┘
              ♠ Q10
              ♡ AK52
              ◇ Q9
              ♣ J8742
```

South	West	North	East
1NT	Pass	3NT	All Pass

Contract: Three No-Trumps by South
Lead: two of spades

West leads the two of spades against South's game. Declarer wins with the queen in hand and plays ace, king and another club. West follows to the first club and then discards the six of spades and the three of hearts. You win your queen and must decide what to do next.

What do you know about West's distribution? When he led the two of spades that marked him with four cards in spades – remember, you lead the fourth highest. Hence he is unlikely to have a five-card suit anywhere, or he would have led it. When he showed out on the second club you could be pretty sure his distribution was 4-4-4-1. When he chose a spade as his first discard, you knew not to return his initial lead; when he discarded a heart he was suggesting weakness in that suit.

If West is 4-4-4-1, then declarer is 2-4-2-5 (you might not approve of his One No-Trump opening but he was worried about having to rebid a poor five-card club suit).

What should you do now? The best chance is to find declarer with most of his values in hearts, in which case a diamond switch looks best, especially if declarer holds only Qx in that suit.

Switch to the ace of diamonds and continue with the jack in order to unblock the suit.

The key to finding the winning switch was working out and counting the distribution of the whole hand.

Lesson 71
First things first

The bidding on this hand may look a little strange to you. Cover up the West and South hands before reading on.

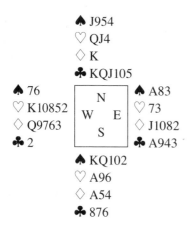

```
            ♠ J954
            ♡ QJ4
            ◇ K
            ♣ KQJ105
♠ 76          N        ♠ A83
♡ K10852   W     E     ♡ 73
◇ Q9763       S        ◇ J1082
♣ 2                    ♣ A943
            ♠ KQ102
            ♡ A96
            ◇ A54
            ♣ 876
```

South	West	North	East
1NT	Pass	2♣	Pass
2♠	Pass	4♠	All Pass

Contract: Four Spades by South
Lead: two of clubs

In Lessons 30 and 31 we told you that a bid in a suit at the two level over One No-Trump showed a weak hand; the opener was expected to pass. This was an over-simplification of what is generally played.

A Two Club response to a One No-Trump opening has a special meaning: it is called the Stayman convention (see Lessons 148 and 149) and it asks partner if he has a four-card major. If he has one he bids it, while if he doesn't he bids Two Diamonds. Generally speaking, if you have the values for game, you are more likely to make it in a 4-4 major-suit fit, if you have one, than in Three No-Trumps.

Here North wanted to discover if South had four spades, so he bid Two Clubs, Stayman. When South bid Two Spades North was happy to raise to Four Spades; if South had bid Two Diamonds or Two Hearts, North would have bid Three No-Trumps.

But, enough of the bidding for the moment. How do you defend as East?

Your partner's two of clubs is clearly a singleton. Do you win and give him a ruff?

If you do, you will have let declarer make his contract. After taking his ruff, partner will play, say, a diamond. Declarer will win and knock out your ace of spades. He will later discard both his hearts on dummy's clubs and make ten tricks.

Because you have the ace of spades you have trump control and need not rush to give partner his ruff. Win the ace of clubs and switch to a heart. Declarer has no choice but to take the finesse. Later you win the first round of trumps with the ace and then give partner a club ruff for the setting trick; the heart ruff partner gives you will mean two down.

This is a very tough hand. The key here, as is so often the case with defence, is counting both the declarer's and the defenders' tricks. Remember, you need to take *four*.

Lesson 72
Communications 1

One important aspect of declarer play and defence is keeping communications open between the two hands. There is no use in one hand having lots of winners if he cannot get the lead. So, try to keep your own communications open and do all you can to sever your opponents'. Cover up the East and South hands before reading on.

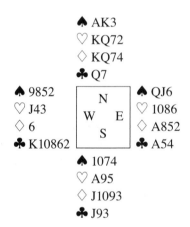

```
              ♠ AK3
              ♡ KQ72
              ◇ KQ74
              ♣ Q7
    ♠ 9852              ♠ QJ6
    ♡ J43     N         ♡ 1086
    ◇ 6    W     E      ◇ A852
    ♣ K10862   S        ♣ A54
              ♠ 1074
              ♡ A95
              ◇ J1093
              ♣ J93
```

South	West	North	East
–	–	1♡	Pass
1NT	Pass	3NT	All Pass

Contract: Three No-Trumps by South
Lead: six of clubs

As West you lead the six of clubs against South's Three No-Trumps. Declarer plays low from dummy and your partner wins with the ace as declarer plays the three.

Partner now returns the five of clubs on which declarer plays the nine. Over to you.

If you win your king you can kiss goodbye to your defence. Although you next clear the clubs you do not have an entry so will not be able to cash your two established winners. The correct play is a low club on the second round. Declarer will win the trick with dummy's queen. Now, in order to succeed, he needs to make the next eight tricks for if your partner ever gains the lead he will play his remaining club back and you will cash three winners in the suit.

And you know that partner has a third club, don't you? In earlier lessons we have explained about leading fourth highest and how that helps partner to count the hand. But it is not only the opening leader who must be helpful. Here if East started with four clubs (or five) he should return his original fourth highest; if he started with three he returns his top one; if he started with two he has only one left to return. After the play to the first two tricks you know partner did not start with four (if so, he would have had AJ95 and would have played the jack at trick one). If he started with A5 alone, then declarer would have had J943 and the nine would have been a strange card to play on the second round.

No, partner must have a third club and to beat the contract he just needs to obtain the lead – and if he can't, then there was no chance of beating the contract whatever you did.

Lesson 73
Communications 2

The most common form of bridge, which is played by people in their own homes (and in some bridge clubs) all over the world, is called rubber bridge. In this game the hands are dealt at the table; to win you need good luck as well as to play well – no-one can win if they never hold any cards. Tournament bridge is different. In this form of the game the same hands are played at more than one table, thus eliminating the luck factor; those who win are those who play better.

This deal occurred in a knock-out teams match.

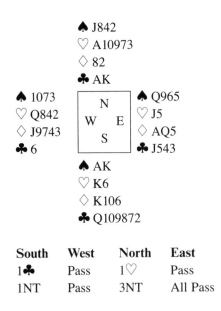

♠ J842			
♡ A10973			
◇ 82			
♣ AK			

South	West	North	East
1♣	Pass	1♡	Pass
1NT	Pass	3NT	All Pass

Contract: Three No-Trumps by South
Lead: four of diamonds

South's hand on this deal is very suitable for no-trump play despite the six-card club suit. Rebidding One No-Trump was the correct action because of the poorish club suit and honours in the short suits. It made for a simple auction to the best game.

Plan the defence.

At one table East won the ace of diamonds and returned the queen. Declarer ducked and won the third round. Now he cashed the ace and king of clubs, crossed back to hand with a spade and gave up a club. East had no more diamonds and could not put his partner in, so declarer eventually made ten tricks.

At the other table, East was more on the ball. Instead of winning the ace of diamonds at trick one he put in the queen. While it would have worked well this time for South to duck that, if West had led from AJxxx he would have looked rather silly, losing the first five tricks when he perhaps had ten on top. So declarer won his king of diamonds and now the defence had to prevail. When East got the lead with jack of clubs he played ace and another diamond and West cashed out (having astutely refrained from discarding a diamond on the clubs) for one down.

Part IV
More on Declarer Play

We looked at some basic declarer play in the section on MiniBridge and, of course, there have been plenty of opportunities to practise in the bidding and defence sections. However, now the time has come to look at some cardplay techniques in more depth.

Lesson 74
Counting as declarer

Counting is just as important in declarer play as it is in defence. You probably do not yet have the confidence in your bidding to bid a grand slam (all thirteen tricks) at the table, so here is one for you to set up for yourself and see how you go. If you are not going to set the deal out for yourself, at least cover up the East-West hands before considering your play.

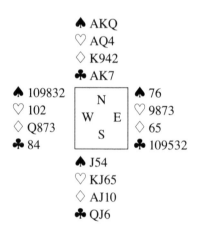

♠ AKQ
♡ AQ4
◇ K942
♣ AK7

♠ 109832
♡ 102
◇ Q873
♣ 84

♠ 76
♡ 9873
◇ 65
♣ 109532

♠ J54
♡ KJ65
◇ AJ10
♣ QJ6

South	West	North	East
1NT	Pass	7NT	All Pass

Contract: Seven No-Trumps by South
Lead: ten of spades

With 25 points facing his partner's 12–14, North was quite justified in bidding the grand slam. Indeed, he was a little unlucky there were not thirteen tricks on top.

A quick count of the tricks available arrives at a total of twelve with a two-way diamond guess available for the thirteenth.

On this type of hand best technique is to put off the crucial decision until the last possible moment in the hope of discovering as much as possible about the distribution of the hand.

Win the spade lead and cash your hearts discarding a diamond from dummy. You discover that West started with a doubleton heart. Now cash two more top spades, discovering that East began with a doubleton spade. Finally cash three rounds of clubs. West had a doubleton in that suit. So, West's initial distribution was 5-2-4-2 and East 2-4-2-5 (when we give a distribution in this way, it is always in the order spades, hearts, diamonds, clubs).

West has four diamonds to East's two and is therefore twice as likely to hold the queen. So, cash the ace of diamonds and run the jack to land your grand slam.

Any missing card is more likely to be in the hand with the length in the suit. A two-way finesse is *always* better than a 50% chance (indeed, some players claim a near 100% record). Always put off such a guess for as long as possible in order to find out all you can about the distribution before making the key play.

Lesson 75
Counting tricks

In the last lesson we looked at a hand where declarer had to count the defenders' distribution. Here what he needs to do is count his own tricks. Set the North-South hands out for yourself before reading on.

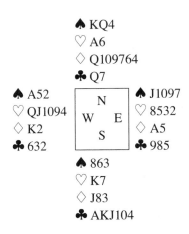

♠ KQ4
♡ A6
◇ Q109764
♣ Q7

♠ A52
♡ QJ1094
◇ K2
♣ 632

♠ J1097
♡ 8532
◇ A5
♣ 985

♠ 863
♡ K7
◇ J83
♣ AKJ104

South	West	North	East
1NT	Pass	3NT	All Pass

Contract: Three No-Trumps by South
Lead: queen of hearts

With only 13 points and a semi-balanced hand there was no point in North looking for a diamond contract; nine tricks are usually much easier than eleven.

West leads the queen of hearts. A declarer who was not paying full attention might easily make the mistake of playing a diamond; after all it is his longest suit and once the ace and king have been knocked out four extra tricks will be generated.

A more alert declarer will work out that there is no time for such a play. The defence will win the first diamond and knock out the remaining heart stopper. Then when they win the next diamond they will have at least three hearts to cash.

Declarer should, as always, start by counting his tricks. He has seven on top, so needs just two more and the best place to find them is in spades. Although his contract is not guaranteed he will make it half the time. All he needs is for West to hold the ace of spades.

Win the first heart in hand and play a spade to the queen. If it holds, cash five rounds of clubs and then play another spade. If West has the ace you have your ninth trick.

When dummy comes down, declarer should start by counting his tricks and also counting his losers. Until he knows how many extra tricks he needs and what losers he has he cannot devise a sensible plan.

Lesson 76
The finesse

The definition of a finesse, according to the *Encyclopedia of Bridge* is: 'The attempt to gain power for lower-ranking cards by taking advantage of the favourable position of high-ranking cards held by the opposition.'

Use your pack of cards to set out and play these combinations before looking at the answers.

A finesse to avoid a loser

Some examples of this are:

(A) AQ   (B) A64
     [   ]   [   ]
     654   QJ10

With (A), if you lead from hand towards dummy's queen, you avoid a loser whenever West has the king. With (B), by running the queen, you also avoid a loser whenever West has the king.

A finesse to promote a winner

Some examples of this are:

(C) K5   (D) A64
     [   ]   [   ]
     64   Q86

If you lead towards the king on (C) you will make a trick whenever West holds the ace. If you play to the ace on (D) and then back to your queen you will make an extra trick whenever East has the king.

A finesse to set up a second finesse

Again, use your pack of cards to set up these examples:

(E) AJ10   (F) AQ10
     [   ]   [   ]
     642   642

(G) Q109   (H) K109
     [   ]   [   ]
     843   843

With (E) you must always lose one trick. Play to the jack, expecting to lose to East. Then, provided West has one honour, another finesse, i.e. play to the ten, will see you with a second trick in the suit. With (F) the principle is similar but here you will make three tricks if West has both the king and jack.

With (G), lead to the nine, hoping to lose to East's ace or king. When you play the suit again, if West plays the ace or king your queen is established; if he plays low you play the ten to force East's remaining top honour. With (H), lead towards dummy and play the nine, which will probably lose to the queen or jack. Next lead another low one to dummy and play the ten, hoping this will force the ace and establish your king.

Lesson 77
Correct handling

Declarer had to be careful about which card to play on the first round of the suit in order to take advantage of the favourable heart position on this hand.

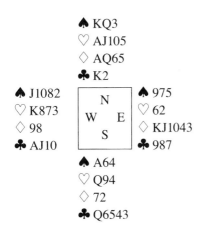

♠ KQ3
♥ AJ105
♦ AQ65
♣ K2

♠ J1082
♥ K873
♦ 98
♣ AJ10

♠ 975
♥ 62
♦ KJ1043
♣ 987

♠ A64
♥ Q94
♦ 72
♣ Q6543

South	West	North	East
–	–	1♥	Pass
1NT	Pass	3NT	All Pass

Contract: Three No-Trumps by South
Lead: jack of spades

North, with his 19 HCP, was much too strong to open One No-Trump, and so started with his four-card major, hearts. South did not have quite enough to respond at the two level, so settled for One No-Trump. With three cards to an honour in hearts and a small doubleton outside, Two Hearts would have been a good alternative, but for the moment it is better for you to have four cards for an immediate raise unless you have a singleton in an outside suit. If North had had 17 or 18 points he would have contented himself with a raise to Two No-Trumps, but with 19 he was worth a jump to game.

Declarer on this deal had just learnt all about finesses. He won the opening lead in hand and ran the queen of hearts successfully. He then played a heart to dummy's ten which also held. He now turned his attention to the club suit by playing the king from the dummy and this held the trick. He played a second club and ducked it, West winning with the jack. West continued with a second spade. Declarer won in dummy and tried a low diamond. East won with the ten and played a third spade. Declarer now took his only chance, that hearts were 3-3, and tried the ace of hearts. When the king did not fall he had to concede defeat. It was well defended by West. By ducking the king of clubs he prevented declarer from reaching his hand to take another heart finesse. Do you see where declarer went wrong?

At trick two, instead of running the queen of hearts he should have run the nine. When that held he could have continued with the queen, after which he would still have been in his own hand to take a third finesse in the suit. Instead of making only three heart tricks, he would have made four which, together with three spades and one trick in each minor, would have been enough for his contract.

Lesson 78
Now or never

In an ideal world we like to put off finessing for as long as possible. After all, if we leave it long enough, an opponent might play the suit for us and we may not need the finesse at all. However, sometimes the only chance is to take the finesse immediately.

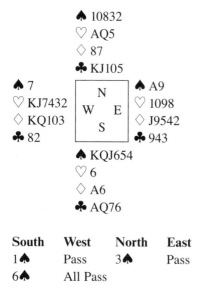

South	**West**	**North**	**East**
1♠	Pass	3♠	Pass
6♠	All Pass		

Contract: Six Spades by South
Lead: king of diamonds

One of the most exciting things you can do in bridge is bid and make a slam. Though we will not cover this topic in depth until Part VI, we thought it a good idea to give you a taste of that excitement now. South showed good evaluation of his hand after his partner gave him a jump raise to Three Spades. In Part VI you will learn how to proceed when you think there may be a slam on.

When West led the king of diamonds and South saw the dummy he realised that he had been a little too enthusiastic. He had to do something about the diamond loser immediately, otherwise he would be one down as soon as an opponent won the ace of spades.

Accordingly, declarer won the ace of diamonds and played a heart to dummy's queen straight away. When it held, he cashed the ace of hearts discarding his diamond and only now did he play a trump. Although this play risked going two down (if East had held the king of hearts), when it succeeded he made his slam.

Notice that if West had led a heart at trick one, declarer would still have had to take a finesse as his only chance to succeed.

Lesson 79
The safe hand 1

Sometimes the order in which you make your plays is critical. Set out the following hand and play it before reading further:

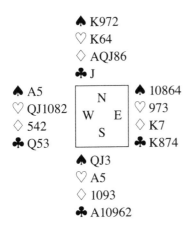

```
            ♠ K972
            ♡ K64
            ◇ AQJ86
            ♣ J
♠ A5          N          ♠ 10864
♡ QJ1082   W     E       ♡ 973
◇ 542         S          ◇ K7
♣ Q53                    ♣ K874
            ♠ QJ3
            ♡ A5
            ◇ 1093
            ♣ A10962
```

South	West	North	East
–	–	1◇	Pass
2NT	Pass	3NT	All Pass

Contract: Three No-Trumps by South
Lead: queen of hearts

West leads the queen of hearts against South's no-trump game. How should South play?

He should start by counting his tricks. He has only four on top and needs to establish winners in both spades and diamonds if he is going to bring his total up to nine.

It is a matter of good general technique to duck the first trick in this type of situation.

If hearts are 6-2, when you later lose a trick to East he will not be able to establish the suit. So, duck the first heart and win the second. What do you do next?

Suppose you take a diamond finesse. East will win and clear the hearts. When you knock out the ace of spades West will win and cash his hearts. Unlucky? You would have been all right if East had had the ace of spades.

Now see what happens if you play a spade first. Say West ducks; you then play a low spade. Although West can establish his hearts he no longer has a quick entry and can't get in to cash them. If he returns a heart you win, cross to hand with a spade and take a diamond finesse. East wins but has no entry to his partner's hand. He will probably try a club but you can win with the ace and cash your diamonds, making nine tricks: two spades, two hearts, four diamonds and one club.

You did not mind who held the ace of spades because that card would be knocked out while both defenders still held hearts. But once your last heart stopper had been knocked out you could only afford to lose to East, who had no hearts left; that was the time to take the diamond finesse. Here East was the safe hand. West was the menacing danger hand.

Lesson 80
The safe hand 2

The theme on this hand is similar to that in Lesson 79:

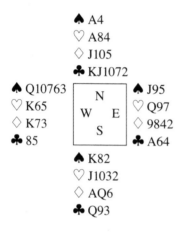

♠ A4
♥ A84
♦ J105
♣ KJ1072

♠ Q10763   ♠ J95
♥ K65   ♥ Q97
♦ K73   ♦ 9842
♣ 85   ♣ A64

♠ K82
♥ J1032
♦ AQ6
♣ Q93

South	West	North	East
1NT	Pass	3NT	All Pass

Contract: Three No-Trumps by South
Lead: six of spades

West led the six of spades and South paused to count his tricks: two in spades, one in hearts and one in diamonds. To arrive at nine he needed to establish four tricks in clubs and one more in diamonds. If West had both the king of diamonds and the ace of clubs there was nothing South could do but if East had the ace of clubs declarer could guarantee success by starting with the diamond finesse.

So, declarer ducked the opening lead, won the spade continuation and led the five of diamonds to his queen. West won the king and continued spades. Declarer won in hand and only now did he play a club. His foresight was rewarded when East turned up with the ace and could not put his partner in to cash the spades. Declarer made two spades, one heart, two diamonds and four clubs.

Note what would have happened if South had started by playing on his longest suit. East would have won the ace of clubs and cleared the spades. Then later on, when declarer took the diamond finesse, West would have won and cashed his spades.

Although it is usually right to play on your long suit first in a no-trump conact, this is by no means always the case. You need to consider the possible distributions of the opposing honours. Always try to knock out the *danger hand*'s entries first (the danger hand is the one who has the long suit).

Lesson 81
Suit establishment

Another key aspect of declarer play is that of suit establishment and entries. If entries are thin on the ground you have to be particularly careful in handling those that you do have.

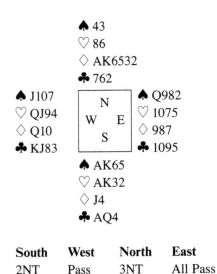

```
            ♠ 43
            ♡ 86
            ◇ AK6532
            ♣ 762
♠ J107                    ♠ Q982
♡ QJ94      N             ♡ 1075
◇ Q10     W   E           ◇ 987
♣ KJ83      S             ♣ 1095
            ♠ AK65
            ♡ AK32
            ◇ J4
            ♣ AQ4
```

South	West	North	East
2NT	Pass	3NT	All Pass

Contract: Three No-Trumps by South
Lead: queen of hearts

We have not yet covered what to do with balanced hands that are stronger than 19 points. But part of the answer is to open Two No-Trumps with 20–22 (see Lesson 128). As after a One No-Trump opening, there is not much point introducing a minor suit unless you are either interested in a slam or are extremely distributional. Here North correctly raised straight to Three No-Trumps.

West led the queen of hearts and declarer paused to take stock. He had seven winners on top. While an eighth could come from a successful club finesse, the most likely source of several tricks was dummy's diamond suit. However, there were communication problems.

If declarer simply plays out his top diamonds he will set up three extra winners in the suit but has no entry to reach them.

Having ducked the first heart and won the second (good technique though it doesn't matter here), now play a low diamond from both hands. Win the heart continuation and play your top diamonds. Provided the suit breaks 3-2 (which happens nearly 70% of the time) you make five diamond tricks and ten tricks in all.

Inexperienced players often worry about ducking tricks. They are afraid they will never make them. This can happen if you duck without purpose, but there are many situations where tricks ducked early come back with interest later on.

Lesson 82
Clues from the bidding 1

The good declarer uses whatever clues he can to work out his opponents' hands. As well as clues from defensive play, there are often clues in the bidding, or lack of it.

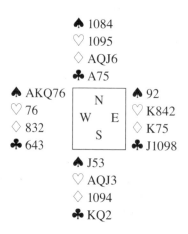

♠ 1084
♡ 1095
◇ AQJ6
♣ A75

♠ AKQ76
♡ 76
◇ 832
♣ 643

♠ 92
♡ K842
◇ K75
♣ J1098

♠ J53
♡ AQJ3
◇ 1094
♣ KQ2

South	West	North	East
–	Pass	Pass	Pass
1NT	Pass	2NT	All Pass

Contract: Two No-Trumps by South
Lead: ace of spades, followed by the king, queen and two other spades

South opened One No-Trump in fourth position and North raised to Two No-Trumps which ended the auction.

When West cashed his five spade tricks, East followed twice and then threw three clubs. What should declarer throw from his hand and dummy?

Surely West would have opened the bidding if he had had a red-suit king to go with his excellent five-card spade suit, so you must work on the assumption that East holds both red-suit kings.

That makes it easy. The eight tricks you will expect to make are three clubs, four hearts and one diamond. You discard two diamonds from each hand. No doubt when West has finished cashing spades he will play a diamond. You rise with dummy's ace and run the ten of hearts. When that holds you take a second heart finesse. Now cash your three club tricks ending in dummy and take a third heart finesse for your contract.

There are several clues to look for in the bidding. Here are a few:

(1) A player who has not opened the bidding when he had the opportunity to do so will usually hold fewer than 12 HCP.

(2) A player who has not *overcalled* at the one level when he is known to have a few values will not usually hold a reasonable five-card major (overcalls, i.e. bids after an opponent has opened, will be discussed in detail in Part V).

(3) A player who has passed his partner's opening bid will usually have fewer than 6 HCP.

Lesson 83
Clues from the bidding 2

For the last few lessons we have been looking at the play in no-trump contracts. Now we will turn our attention to the play in suits.

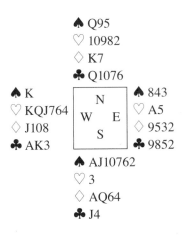

```
              ♠ Q95
              ♡ 10982
              ◇ K7
              ♣ Q1076
  ♠ K           N        ♠ 843
  ♡ KQJ764   W     E     ♡ A5
  ◇ J108                 ◇ 9532
  ♣ AK3         S        ♣ 9852
              ♠ AJ10762
              ♡ 3
              ◇ AQ64
              ♣ J4
```

South	West	North	East
–	1♡	Pass	Pass
1♠	2♡	2♠	Pass
4♠	All Pass		

Contract: Four Spades by South
Lead: king of hearts – East overtakes with the ace and plays another heart, West winning and continuing with a third heart

We have not yet covered competitive bidding which is usually based more on distribution than on high cards. Here South overcalls One Spade after both North and East have passed. As we will see later, this *protective* bid can be made on a wide range of hands. North made a token raise and South went straight to game based on his good distribution.

West leads the king of hearts which East overtakes with the ace to play a second heart, ruffed by declarer. Since East has shown up with the ace of hearts and could not find a bid over his partner's One Heart opening it seems certain that West holds the king of spades; if that is the case the only hope is that it is singleton, because declarer cannot afford a spade loser to go with the heart and two clubs.

So, at trick three declarer laid down the ace of spades and was no doubt pleased to see West's king drop. Declarer now drew the rest of the trumps and played the jack of clubs. West won and continued a heart. Declarer ruffed and played another club. Again West won and forced out declarer's last trump but the queen of clubs was established in the dummy for a diamond discard.

Of course, East should have allowed West's king of hearts to hold trick one, leaving some doubt as to the location of the ace. West should now switch to the jack of diamonds. Declarer could now be forgiven for taking the spade finesse.

Lesson 84
Drawing trumps

One of the problems that declarer has to solve when playing in a suit contract is when to draw trumps. If declarer counts his tricks properly he should usually be able to come up with the right answer.

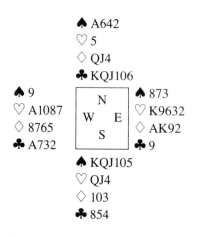

```
              ♠ A642
              ♡ 5
              ◇ QJ4
              ♣ KQJ106
  ♠ 9                      ♠ 873
  ♡ A1087    N             ♡ K9632
  ◇ 8765   W   E           ◇ AK92
  ♣ A732     S             ♣ 9
              ♠ KQJ105
              ♡ QJ4
              ◇ 103
              ♣ 854
```

South	West	North	East
–	–	1♣	1♡
1♠	3♡	3♠	All Pass

Contract: Three Spades by South
Lead: nine of spades

Although East-West have fewer than half the points in the pack it is their side that can make game on this deal. They stopped short, however, and North-South were allowed to buy the hand in Three Spades.

You might think that South, with 9 points, should proceed to Four Spades over Three Spades. However, he correctly recognised that: (a) North might have had to stretch to bid Three Spades, and (b) his QJx of hearts were of little use when North probably had a singleton.

West decided to lead a trump, hoping to cut down ruffs. It is tempting for declarer to go after heart ruffs, but look what might happen on the actual deal. East wins his king of hearts and play his singleton club. Now a club ruff goes with a heart, two diamonds and a club to beat Three Spades.

The heart ruffs are a red herring. All declarer need do is win the trump lead, draw trumps and play a club. West wins and the best he can do now is play a diamond for East to take his two tricks in the suit, otherwise declarer will make at least ten tricks.

When playing in a suit contract it is a good idea to start off by imagining that you are in no-trumps and work out if you have the required number of tricks without doing any ruffing. If your tally falls short, then you can consider how ruffing might help.

Lesson 85
Taking ruffs

This hand, although in some ways similar to the one in the previous lesson, shows how taking ruffs in the dummy can be the easiest route to the required number of tricks.

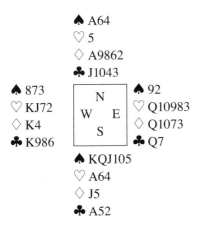

```
              ♠ A64
              ♡ 5
              ◇ A9862
              ♣ J1043
♠ 873                      ♠ 92
♡ KJ72      N              ♡ Q10983
◇ K4     W     E           ◇ Q1073
♣ K986      S              ♣ Q7
              ♠ KQJ105
              ♡ A64
              ◇ J5
              ♣ A52
```

South	West	North	East
1♠	Pass	2◇	Pass
2NT	Pass	3♠	Pass
4♠	All Pass		

Contract: Four Spades by South
Lead: seven of spades

This was a good bidding sequence by North-South. Over South's One Spade North had the values for a two-level response. South rebid Two No-Trumps to show 15–17 points and a balanced hand. Now North showed three-card spade support and South chose game in the major suit.

West led the seven of spades. If, as we recommended in the last lesson, declarer counts his tricks as if he were in a no-trump contract, he arrives at a total of eight, two short of his target. If declarer uses his small trumps in dummy to ruff his two heart losers, this will bring his total up to ten.

The straightforward line is to win the ace of spades, play a heart to the ace and ruff a heart, play a club to the ace and ruff another heart. Five tricks in the bag with the ace of diamonds and KQJ10 of spades still to come.

Not all hands are this easy to count, of course. When in doubt it generally pays to put off drawing trumps. After all, you have chosen to play in your trump suit because you have more than the opponents and it is not so likely that they will be able to ruff in and upset your plans.

Lesson 86
Severing communications

Some of the ducking plays that we have looked at when considering the play in no-trumps can be applied just as well in a suit contract. This hand is a straightforward example:

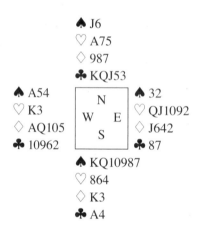

North:
♠ J6
♡ A75
◇ 987
♣ KQJ53

West:
♠ A54
♡ K3
◇ AQ105
♣ 10962

East:
♠ 32
♡ QJ1092
◇ J642
♣ 87

South:
♠ KQ10987
♡ 864
◇ K3
♣ A4

South	West	North	East
–	1NT	Pass	2♡
2♠	Pass	3♠	Pass
4♠	All Pass		

Contract: Four Spades by South
Lead: king of hearts

Aggressive bidding by North-South got them a little high on this deal; both of them thought the other was likely to be short in hearts. Still, when West led the king of hearts the contract was virtually 100%.

The thoughtless declarer would just grab the ace of hearts and play a trump. West would win and play a heart to his partner's jack. East would cash another heart and play a diamond through: two down.

A better line is to duck the king of hearts and win the heart continuation. Now when West wins his ace of trumps he has no more hearts to play. Not only have you restricted his heart tricks to one, you have also denied East the entry he needed to push a diamond through your king. In the fullness of time declarer can discard his remaining red-suit losers on dummy's good clubs.

When you have Axx facing two or three small cards it is very often right to duck at trick one. If the defending hands were sufficiently distributional for them to get a ruff it is likely that they would have bid. The duck is often crucial to severing their communications.

Lesson 87
Suit establishment in a suit contract

When you have good long suits in one hand or the other (usually dummy) it can be just as important to set them up when you are in a suit contract as when you are in no-trumps. Don't forget your pack of cards.

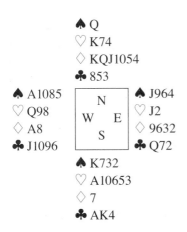

```
              ♠ Q
              ♡ K74
              ◇ KQJ1054
              ♣ 853
♠ A1085                    ♠ J964
♡ Q98       N              ♡ J2
◇ A8      W   E            ◇ 9632
♣ J1096       S            ♣ Q72
              ♠ K732
              ♡ A10653
              ◇ 7
              ♣ AK4
```

South	West	North	East
1♡	Pass	2◇	Pass
2♡	Pass	3♡	Pass
4♡	All Pass		

Contract: Four Hearts by South
Lead: jack of clubs

South had one of those hands where rebidding a poor five-card suit was unavoidable (see Lesson 48 on reverses).

Declarer has two aces to lose and most likely a trump trick. In addition, the defenders are threatening to set up a club winner.

A declarer who was only interested in losers might win the club lead and play a spade. West would win the ace and continue with clubs. Declarer would win the ace, cash the king of spades discarding a club and ruff a club in the dummy. Now he would have to play a diamond. West would win his ace and play, say, another spade. Declarer ruffs, cashes the king of hearts and plays a diamond discarding his last spade. In dummy he has nothing left but diamonds and his hand is all trumps. When he plays a diamond and ruffs in hand, West overruffs and plays the thirteenth club. East ruffs with the jack, forcing declarer to overruff with the ace and promoting a trump trick for West's queen.

Where declarer went wrong is that this hand is not about losers, it is about winners. Dummy has a huge source of tricks in diamonds and declarer must be sure to take advantage of this. All declarer needs do is play a diamond at trick two. He wins the club return, cashes the ace and king of trumps and runs diamonds, letting the defenders make a heart trick and the ace of spades whenever they like.

Lesson 88
Preserving entries

The best way to learn from these lessons is to deal out the North-South cards and work out how you would play before reading on. If circumstances do not permit this, just plan your play without looking at the East-West cards.

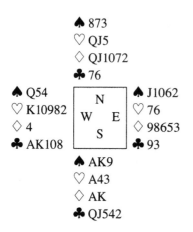

```
                ♠ 873
                ♡ QJ5
                ◇ QJ1072
                ♣ 76
  ♠ Q54      ┌───────┐   ♠ J1062
  ♡ K10982   │   N   │   ♡ 76
  ◇ 4        │ W   E │   ◇ 98653
  ♣ AK108    │   S   │   ♣ 93
             └───────┘
                ♠ AK9
                ♡ A43
                ◇ AK
                ♣ QJ542
```

South	West	North	East
–	1♡	Pass	Pass
2NT	Pass	3NT	All Pass

Contract: Three No-Trumps by South
Lead: ten of hearts

In a later lesson (122) we will see that a One No-Trump overcall in the fourth position shows about 12–15 points. With 16–18 you double and then bid no-trumps, but with 19–21 you jump straight to Two No-Trumps. (In second position, i.e. directly over the opening bid, all these actions show stronger hands).

Plan the play on the ten of hearts lead.

The straightforward, reflex line is to play the queen of hearts from dummy. When that holds the trick you might play a club to your jack and West's king. West has a number of ways to defend now, all of which will be successful to some degree or other. Best is for him to switch to the queen of spades. But, suppose he even continues with a second heart. You win in dummy and play another club. He wins and clears the hearts. It is hard to see how you will make more than two spades, three hearts and two diamonds.

As is often the case, the secret is in the play to trick one. When dummy comes down you should count your tricks: five diamonds, two spades and two hearts. But in order to reach your diamond tricks you need an entry to dummy *after* you have unblocked the ace and king from your hand.

Instead of playing an honour from dummy at trick one, play low and win in hand with your ace. Now cash the ace and king of diamonds and play a second heart. Whether West plays his king or not, dummy cannot be denied an entry and you will make nine tricks easily.

Lesson 89
Yet more on suit establishment

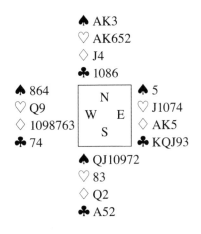

♠ AK3
♡ AK652
◇ J4
♣ 1086

♠ 864   ♠ 5
♡ Q9   ♡ J1074
◇ 1098763   ◇ AK5
♣ 74   ♣ KQJ93

♠ QJ10972
♡ 83
◇ Q2
♣ A52

South	West	North	East
–	–	–	1♣
1♠	Pass	4♠	All Pass

Contract: Four Spades by South.
Lead: seven of clubs

Although South has only 9 HCP, with a good six-card suit it is clear to overcall One Spade; overcalls are about playing strength and good suits rather than points. If South had opened One Spade, North would have bid Two Hearts. Such a bid would have been forcing for one round. North would have wanted to ascertain that South had five spades before raising the suit; he would also have had some thoughts of slam had South shown an above-minimum opener. Here, when South has overcalled One Spade, it is best to go straight to Four Spades: South is

known to have a five-card suit for an overcall, and slam is unlikely once East has opened.

Cover up the East and West hands and plan the play before reading on.

You have six spade tricks, two hearts and a club. Your only real chance of establishing the extra trick you need is to set up dummy's hearts. Suppose you draw trumps in three rounds and play the ace and king of hearts and ruff a heart. You will go down if hearts break 4-2 (which happens most of the time), for, although you can cross to dummy with a trump to ruff out the suit, you have no entry back to reach your established winner.

You should have started to set up hearts earlier. Win the opening lead, cash the queen of spades (you can afford one round of trumps) and the two top hearts and ruff a heart high. Now cross to a trump and ruff another heart high. Finally cross back again with a trump and cash your long heart. Note that if hearts were 5-1 you had no hope of making your contract, so it could not cost to play hearts before drawing trumps.

Lesson 90
The ruffing finesse

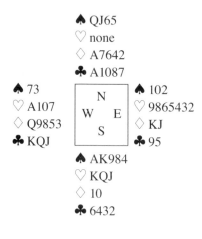

                ♠ QJ65
                ♡ none
                ◇ A7642
                ♣ A1087

♠ 73   N   ♠ 102
♡ A107   W   E   ♡ 9865432
◇ Q9853   S   ◇ KJ
♣ KQJ   ♣ 95

                ♠ AK984
                ♡ KQJ
                ◇ 10
                ♣ 6432

South	West	North	East
1♠	Pass	6♠	All Pass

Contract: Six Spades by South
Lead: king of clubs

North's direct leap to Six Spades over his partner's One Spade opening may look odd but he was playing in a scratch partnership with few agreed conventions. He took the view that, with his three first-round controls and good four-card trump support, there should be reasonable play for slam.

Decide what line you would adopt before reading on.

At the table declarer did not give the hand enough thought. He won the ace of clubs and simply embarked on a cross-ruff. Eventually he ran out of tricks and went two down.

You should quickly reject the cross-ruff as a possible line. With only two outside winners, even if you made all your nine trumps separately you would be a trick short. The solution lies in the honour combination in hearts. All you need is for West to hold the ace.

The twelve tricks you must hope for are: five spades in hand, two minor-suit aces, two hearts once you have ruffed out West's ace and three ruffs in the dummy.

Win the ace of clubs, cash the ace of diamonds and ruff a diamond. Now play the king of hearts. Say West covers with the ace (if he doesn't you discard a club from dummy and continue with the queen of hearts). You ruff in dummy, ruff another diamond and cash the queen and jack of hearts discarding two clubs from the dummy. Now give up a club. Whatever West returns you can cross-ruff the last four tricks. Note that it was important not to draw a single round of trumps earlier. Otherwise West could have played a second trump when he won his club trick and on some lay-outs that would have been fatal.

On the actual club lead, the ruffing heart finesse needed to be right. Had West led a diamond, however, declarer wins, ruffs a diamond and runs the king of hearts, discarding a club if West plays low. If East can win the ace, declarer throws dummy's remaining two low clubs on the queen and jack of hearts and cross-ruffs as before.

Lesson 91
The double ruffing finesse

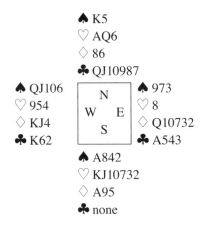

♠ K5
♥ AQ6
♦ 86
♣ QJ10987

♠ QJ106
♥ 954
♦ KJ4
♣ K62

N
W E
S

♠ 973
♥ 8
♦ Q10732
♣ A543

♠ A842
♥ KJ10732
♦ A95
♣ none

South	West	North	East
–	–	1♣	Pass
1♥	Pass	2♣	Pass
2♠	Pass	4♥	Pass
6♥	All Pass		

Contract: Six Hearts by South
Lead: queen of spades

This was a good auction by North. He first rebid his good six-card club suit but when South showed at least invitational values with five hearts and four spades he took a second look at his 12 points: his heart support was the best South could possibly hope for and his king in South's second suit was also likely to be useful. South got carried away at this point; a void in his partner's main suit was a dstinct disadvantage. On a diamond lead the slam would have gone down. However, the defence do not always find the best attack.

Plan the play on the queen of spades lead. A quick count of your tricks reaches only nine: two spades, six hearts and a diamond. Two spade ruffs in the dummy bring the total up to eleven. There is some chance that you could score a diamond ruff as well but when you lose the lead, all the defenders have to do is play a trump to foil that plan.

No, there is a way to generate the extra tricks that simply needs East to have at least one of the top club honours.

Win the king of spades in dummy and play the queen of clubs. If East plays low (it does not help him to play his ace), you discard a diamond and West wins his king, Suppose West continues with a second spade. You win in hand, play a heart to dummy's queen and the jack of clubs. If East covers, you ruff, draw trumps ending in dummy, and cash your clubs. It is better defence for East to duck the jack of clubs. Now you discard your last losing diamond and revert to your plan of ruffing two spades in the dummy. It may look appealing to continue with the ten of clubs, but if you do that West may score a ruff.

Lesson 92
A two-way finesse

North has a tricky bidding problem on this hand.

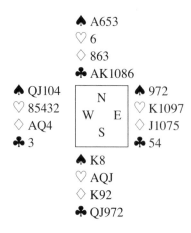

♠ A653
♡ 6
◇ 863
♣ AK1086

♠ QJ104
♡ 85432
◇ AQ4
♣ 3

♠ 972
♡ K1097
◇ J1075
♣ 54

♠ K8
♡ AQJ
◇ K92
♣ QJ972

South	West	North	East
1♣	Pass	1♠	Pass
1NT	Pass	5♣	All Pass

Contract: Five Clubs by South
Lead: queen of spades

When South rebid One No-Trump to show 15–17 points, North knew that his side had the values for game (or even slam) but which game? Three No-Trumps or Five Clubs? Without any fancy methods, North had to guess and he went for the minor-suit game. Although he was wrong this time, in that Three No-Trumps would have been much easier, it is hard to be too critical and Five Clubs certainly has excellent play.

Cover up the East and West hands and make your plan before reading on.

Declarer had recently read the lesson on the ruffing finesse. He won the spade lead, drew trumps, cashed the ace of hearts and ran the queen of hearts (discarding a diamond from dummy) to East's king. However, East switched to the jack of diamonds and the defence took the next two tricks. South felt a little aggrieved when his newly learned play failed him.

It is important to play the whole hand rather than one suit in isolation. Here South would have succeeded had West held the king of hearts, but there is a play that succeeds whoever holds that card.

Declarer should have counted his tricks. All he had to do was win the lead, draw trumps and simply play a heart from dummy to his queen. If it holds the trick, he discards a diamond on the ace of hearts, ruffs a heart in dummy and plays a diamond towards his king, making an overtrick if East holds the ace. If the queen of hearts loses to West's king, West can do him no harm. Declarer wins the return and later discards two diamonds from dummy on the ace and jack of hearts. He loses just one heart and one diamond.

Lesson 93
Lead up to your honours

This hand uses some of what we hope you have learned over the past few lessons. Don't forget to deal out the hand.

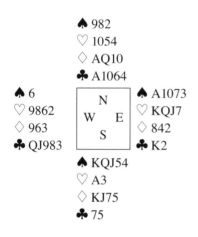

```
              ♠ 982
              ♡ 1054
              ◇ AQ10
              ♣ A1064
♠ 6                        ♠ A1073
♡ 9862        N            ♡ KQJ7
◇ 963      W     E         ◇ 842
♣ QJ983       S            ♣ K2
              ♠ KQJ54
              ♡ A3
              ◇ KJ75
              ♣ 75
```

South	West	North	East
1♠	Pass	2♣	Pass
2◇	Pass	3♠	Pass
4♠	All Pass		

Contract: Four Spades by South
Lead: eight of hearts

North, with his 10 HCP, is worth a two-level response. When South rebids Two Diamonds, North's useful holding in that suit, along with his three-card spade support, justifies a jump to Three Spades; South is happy to go for the vulnerable game.

A trick count reveals that declarer must try to make four spades, one heart, four diamonds and one club, a total of ten. The losers will be a spade, a heart and a club. Can you see any problems?

The danger is if trumps are not 3-2. If West has four trumps including the ace and ten, or if he has bare ace, nothing can be done, but if East has A10xx in trumps, a second trump loser can be avoided provided declarer leads trumps from the dummy. This, then, is the correct sequence of plays.

To start with, you should duck the heart lead. (Suppose West had, say, A10x in spades and a doubleton heart. If you won the lead and played a spade, West would win and play a second heart. East would win and play a third heart, and now West would make a second trump trick whether you ruffed high or low – a *trump promotion*.) Win the second heart, cross to dummy with a diamond and play a spade towards your hand. If it holds, cross back to dummy with a club and play a second spade. When West shows out, cross to dummy with a second diamond and play a third spade. This sequence of plays restricts East to one trump trick and you make your contract.

Lesson 94
Timing

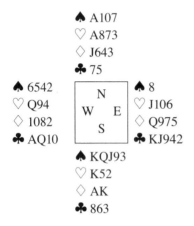

```
                    ♠ A107
                    ♡ A873
                    ◇ J643
                    ♣ 75
    ♠ 6542      ┌─────────┐    ♠ 8
    ♡ Q94       │    N    │    ♡ J106
    ◇ 1082      │  W   E  │    ◇ Q975
    ♣ AQ10      │    S    │    ♣ KJ942
                └─────────┘
                    ♠ KQJ93
                    ♡ K52
                    ◇ AK
                    ♣ 863
```

South	West	North	East
1♠	Pass	2♠	Pass
3♣	Pass	4♠	All Pass

Contract: Four Spades by South
Lead: four of spades

North-South had a good auction on today's hand. Although beginners are taught that they need four-card support to raise partner's One of a major to Two, as they become more experienced they realise that some hands with only three-card support are also suitable for an immediate raise: for example, hands with a singleton or low doubleton in a side-suit.

After the raise to Two Spades, the South hand is worth a try for game. In this type of position, you should bid a suit where you need some help. Here South is right to choose Three Clubs because he needs North to have either shortage or a good honour holding in that suit. This is called a *trial bid*. With two aces and a doubleton club, it is clear for North to accept.

Plan the play on a trump lead.

That trump lead is annoying. Without it your tenth trick would have been a club ruff in dummy. As it is, surely the defenders will continue with trumps every time they win a club. You will have to come up with something else.

You appear to have two chances: the queen of diamonds coming down in three or a 3-3 heart break. At the table declarer played ace, king and another heart immediately. When the suit broke 3-3 he thought he was home but when trumps were 4-1, after drawing trumps he could not reach his established winner.

The correct play is to win the trump lead in hand and duck a heart. Win the trump return in hand, cash the ace and king of diamonds, cross to dummy with a trump to the ace, and ruff a diamond to see if the queen drops. When it doesn't, draw the last trump and try the hearts: the king first, then the ace and finally dummy's established eight.

Part V
Competitive Bidding

Although we covered a lot of bidding situations in Part II, we dealt only with 'constructive' bidding, i.e. bidding between opener and responder with no opposition interference. Of course, in real life both sides are allowed to bid and, very often, they do. This section is all about how to bid when the opposition are bidding too.

We will start with a detailed explanation of the scoring.

Lesson 95
Scoring

Many bridge teachers introduce scoring early on, but in our opinion it is easier to understand after you have been playing for a while.

We explained the concept of 'game' in MiniBridge. To recap, game is Three No-Trumps, Four Hearts or Spades, or Five Clubs or Diamonds. You do not have to make game all in one go. For example, if you bid and make Two Hearts you score 60 (2x30) points. If on the next hand you again bid and make Two Hearts you score another 60 points, a total in excess of 100. That would be a game.

The idea is to win a rubber, which is the best of three games. Here is a typical score sheet (from North-South's viewpoint):

We	They
	500
40 (7)	30 (6)
300 (3)	200 (5)
30 (1)	30 (2)
120 (1)	
80 (4)	60 (2)
	40 (6)
40 (7)	100 (8)

(1) North-South bid Four Spades and made an overtrick. They score 4x30 for their contract. Because that is a making contract it is scored below the line. The overtrick is scored above the line. Since a game has been made, a line is drawn under that score.

(2) East-West bid Two Hearts and make an overtrick. That is 2x30 below the line for their contract. The overtrick scores 30 above the line.

(3) East-West are doubled in Two Spades, and go two light. Doubled undertricks non-vulnerable (see next lesson) score 100 for the first, 200 for the next two and 300 thereafter, hence two down is 300.

(4) North-South bid Four Clubs and make it exactly; 4x20.

(5) North-South bid Four Spades, get doubled and go one down. Vulnerable doubled undertricks score 200 for the first and 300 for each subsequent trick.

(6) East-West bid One No-Trump and make an overtrick; 40 below the line for making One No-Trump and 30 above for the overtrick. They have now scored 60+40=100 below the line, which is game. A line is drawn beneath that score.

(7) North-South bid Two Diamonds and make two overtricks; 2x20 below the line and 2x20 above. They cannot add this to the previous 80 because East-West have made a game.

(8) East-West bid Three No-Trump and make it exactly; 40+30+30=100 below the line for making Three No-Trump.

East-West have now won the rubber and score a bonus of 500. Had North-South not made their game, East-West would have have scored 700. East-West's total is 960 to North-South's 610; a difference of 350 points. This is usually rounded in favour of the losing side. So, if you were playing for, say, 10p a hundred, 30p would change hands.

Lesson 96
Vulnerability and competitive bidding

Vulnerability

When we introduced you to scoring in the last lesson, we touched upon the subject of *vulnerability*. When one side makes a game, and need only one more game for rubber, they are said to be *vulnerable*. The vulnerability makes little difference to the bidding when only one side is in the auction (though some pairs like to play a weak no-trump when non-vulnerable and a strong no-trump vulnerable). However, when the high cards are more evenly divided between the two sides, the vulnerability becomes more significant. While it is important to get into the auction for many reasons, if you choose the wrong moment you may get doubled and suffer a penalty. And doubled undertricks score a lot more if you are vulnerable than if you are not. In simple terms, the more vulnerable you are the more careful you should be. If you are vulnerable and your opponents are not, you need good playing strength in order to enter the auction; if they are vulnerable and you are not you should feel free to take some liberties because their mistakes cost more than yours.

Competitive bidding

Until now all our talk of bidding has assumed that the opponents don't join in, and that you are allowed an uninterrupted conversation. In real life that is not the case. All four players at the table are allowed to bid, and frequently do. If your right-hand opponent opens the bidding you are not obliged to pass; you may make an overcall in a suit or no-trumps, or you may make a take-out double (as distinct from a penalty double – more help on this distinction will follow shortly).

There are three questions to answer:

(1) Why do you wish to compete in the auction?
(2) How do overcalls differ from opening bids?
(3) How do you enter the auction to achieve the best result?

The fact that your right-hand opponent (RHO) makes an opening bid flashes a warning: he has opening-bid values (say 13 HCP), which immediately reduces the total number of HCP your partnership can hold. But say you also hold 13 HCP, this leaves only 14 HCP shared between the two responding partners. At this stage you don't know how those HCP are distributed so you compete to find out which of three possibilities exists:

(1) Your partner has most of the balance, so you might well make game
(2) Opener's partner has most of the balance, so they should outbid you, but at least partner knows which suit you would like led
(3) They are split fairly evenly, so a partscore either way is most likely

Lesson 97
Simple overcalls

The commonest and most straight-forward way to enter the bidding after your right-hand opponent has opened is to make a simple overcall in a new suit.

You do not need opening-bid values, but if you have a reasonable five-card suit to call as trumps you may make a simple overcall at the one level (e.g. 1♡ – 1♠) on as little as 9 or 10 HCP. But if the opening bid is, say, One Heart and your good suit is clubs, you should not overcall at the two level e.g. 1♡ – 2♣ unless you have a six-card suit or significant extra values.

The following hands would all be suitable to overcall One Spade over your RHO's One Heart:

(A)	♠ KQJ95	(B)	♠ KQ5432
	♡ J65		♡ AJ5
	◇ 6		◇ 65
	♣ Q1076		♣ 87

(C)	♠ KQ952	(D)	♠ A10732
	♡ 7		♡ KJ3
	◇ AQ65		◇ Q972
	♣ KJ6		♣ 3

You overcall for several reasons:

(1) To reach your own making partscore or game.
It is unlikely that you will have more high-card points than your opponents once they have opened the bidding, so if you are going to reach your own making contract it will be because you have good playing strength (i.e. distribution) rather than high-card points.

(2) To interfere with your opponents' bidding
Although it is a good idea to try to interfere with your opponents' bidding, because your left-hand opponent (LHO) has heard his partner open the bidding he is in a good position to double you for penalties when that is right for his side. To protect against this you need a good suit to make an overcall.

(3) To help your partner with his defence to the opponents' contract – particularly in his choice of opening lead.
If your partner is going to lead your suit, then it had better be a good one or he may have done better to lead his own.

(4) To pave the way for a possible sacrifice bid
If your opponents can make a game or a slam it may profit your side to bid beyond that level, knowing that you will go down, but that the penalty you will lose will be less than the value of their contract. This is more common when they are vulnerable and you are not.

Lesson 98
Overcalling at the one or two level

You should have a whole extra playing trick to overcall at the two level. Consider these hands after your RHO has opened One Diamond:

(A)	♠ K10652	(B)	♠ A4
	♡ A4		♡ A65
	◇ A65		◇ 763
	♣ 76		♣ K10652
(C)	♠ A4	(D)	♠ A3
	♡ A65		♡ 8765
	◇ 76		◇ 6
	♣ K106542		♣ KQ10954

Hand (A) is a perfectly respectable One Spade overcall at any vulnerability and may enable your partnership to reach its own contract. (Always remember the value of spades – when you hold the highest-ranking suit you can outbid your opponents without raising the level.) With Hand (B) reject a two-level overcall – partner will expect more from you. Don't overcall at the two level without a six-card suit. There are a few exceptions but for the moment we will ignore them. Hand (C) would be acceptable, while Hand (D) is much more suitable because the suit is better – overcall Two Clubs on either of these two hands whatever the vulnerability.

There is the world of difference between a one-level and a two-level overcall. A one-level overcall is, by definition, in a higher-ranking suit than your opponents' so you can outbid them without raising the bidding level. One-level overcalls are more speculative and don't promise opening values.

A two-level overcall is another matter altogether. Because the overcall is in a lower-ranking suit you are less likely to be able to outbid your opponents. As you are a level higher the opponents will be quicker to penalise you. If partner has a good hand he will expect good playing strength. He may well strain to bid Three No-Trumps, expecting you to have a good source of tricks. Alternatively, he may sacrifice over the opponents' game contract. Except in very rare circumstances, you should have at least a six-card suit for a two-level overcall.

What would you bid on the following hands after a One Heart opening bid?

(E)	♠ K542	(F)	♠ J762
	♡ A63		♡ 5
	◇ 5		◇ 64
	♣ AK763		♣ AKJ1054

On Hand (E), despite your 14 HCP you should not overcall Two Clubs. The risks are too high. Hand (F), on the other hand, has only 9 HCP but is worth an overcall at any vulnerability. Your suit is so good that the opponents are unlikely to penalise you. The 6-4 distribution gives the hand greater playing strength. Overcall Two Clubs.

Lesson 99
Putting it into practice

Sitting South, second to speak at Game All, you pick up the following hand:

♠ KQJ102
♡ 42
◇ A7653
♣ 6

Although you have only 10 HCP, this hand would be an opening bid at any vulnerability and position. Two five-card suits are worth at least a couple of high-card points. In addition, you have an excellent spade suit which you would be happy to rebid should partner respond Two Hearts. However, such an opening bid is to be denied you because your RHO opens One Heart. You overcall One Spade and rather to your surprise, that ends the auction. West leads the six of hearts and this is what you see:

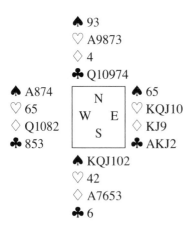

♠ 93
♡ A9873
◇ 4
♣ Q10974

♠ A874   ♠ 65
♡ 65   ♡ KQJ10
◇ Q1082   ◇ KJ9
♣ 853   ♣ AKJ2

♠ KQJ102
♡ 42
◇ A7653
♣ 6

Contract: One Spade by South
Lead: six of hearts

This lowly contract is one where it is particularly important to count your tricks. You have four spades and two aces. You can see that one diamond ruff in the dummy will bring your total up to seven, just what you need for your contract. Don't give the defenders a chance to switch to trumps. Win the ace of hearts, play a diamond to your ace, ruff a diamond and play the nine of spades. Seven tricks are certain. If you start fiddling about trying to make more you may well find you make only six.

You were rather lucky to be allowed to rest in One Spade. East, with his 18 HCP, was rather pusillanimous to let the auction die. That was probably because he did not know what to bid. We will discuss this type of auction later in Lesson 116 (where, believe it or not, you will learn that your correct action is double), but for the moment it would not be unreasonable for him to have bid One No-Trump when One Spade was passed round to him. Although he has no spade stopper, he does have a balanced 18-count and North's failure to raise spades suggests that West has some length/strength in the suit.

Lesson 100
Responding to overcalls 1

When responding to an overcall you should be much more ready to raise your partner's suit than if he had opened the bidding. This is for several reasons:

(1) You know he has a good five-card suit so you need only three-card support to raise him.
(2) Your partner has begun to make life difficult for your opponents, so if you possibly can it is a good idea to continue his good work by bidding vigorously and trying to push them too high.
(3) Raising partner's suit will encourage him to lead it so strain to raise when you have an honour.

Consider the following hands after the bidding sequence: 1♡ – 1♠ – Pass – ?

(A) ♠ K108
  ♡ 82
  ◇ K10743
  ♣ 543

(B) ♠ 543
  ♡ 82
  ◇ K10743
  ♣ K108

With Hand (A) you have a perfect minimum hand for a raise to Two Spades, but on Hand (B) you should pass. On Hand (A) you would welcome a spade lead against an opposing heart or no-trump contract, but on Hand (B) it could well give away a trick. If you were slightly stronger you would have to raise but with a marginal hand it is better

to pass with no spade honour. You may be able to bid Two Spades next time and partner should then realise that your support is weak.

(C) ♠ A1087
  ♡ 82
  ◇ K10743
  ♣ 54

(D) ♠ A10876
  ♡ 8
  ◇ K10743
  ♣ 54

Hand (C) is fine for a raise to Three Spades. When you know partner has a five-card suit you need fewer high cards to raise him when you have four-card support. With Hand (D) you can go the whole hog – bid Four Spades. When you know your side has a ten-card spade fit it is usually right to bid to Four Spades as quickly as possible.

(E) ♠ A1087
  ♡ 842
  ◇ K107
  ♣ 543

(F) ♠ Q43
  ♡ 742
  ◇ AK1054
  ♣ 54

Although the high-card strength and honour location on Hand (E) is identical to Hand (C), the 4-3-3-3 distribution should put you off. You have no ruffing values (i.e. there is no suit that partner will be able to ruff in your hand). Settle for a quiet Two Spades. On Hand (F), if partner had opened One Spade you would have bid Two Diamonds, but here it is better to raise to Two Spades straight away.

Lesson 101
Responding to overcalls 2

Of course, sometimes you have no support for partner but have fair values and need to find an alternative bid. Here we are going to look at two other responses: first, a One No-Trump response and then a bid in a new suit.

A One No-Trump response to an overcall

If partner opens One of a suit, you assume he has 12 HCP. Since he may also have as many as 19 HCP you need to make a response with as little as 6 HCP. When he overcalls you can only assume about 9 HCP and his upper range is about 16 HCP. (We will look at what to do with stronger hands later.) So, if a One No-Trump response to an opening bid is 6–9, then a One No-Trump response to an overcall should be 9–12. Consider the following hands after the sequence 1♡ – 1♠ – Pass – ?

(A)♠ 7	(B)♠ 87
♡ KQ104	♡ AQ5
◇ KJ5	◇ KJ65
♣ 109754	♣ Q1064

Hand (A) is minimum but One No-Trump is a sensible shot with such good hearts and only a singleton in spades. Hand (B) is maximum for One No-Trump but still there is no need for any more vigorous action.

With a stronger hand, say 13–14, you can respond Two No-Trumps and with 15 or more Three No-Trumps.

A bid in a new suit in response to an overcall

Although some partnerships use different methods, we recommend that you play a bid in a new suit as constructive, showing interest in higher things, but not forcing, i.e. partner may pass with a minimum and no fit. Consider the following hands after the auction 1♡ – 1♠ – Pass – ?

(C)♠ 7	(D)♠ 93
♡ 7652	♡ AQ10
◇ QJ10963	◇ KJ762
♣ 65	♣ Q62

Hand (C) is too weak for a response. Even if diamonds plays better, partner may bid too high if you bid the suit. On Hand (D) your suit is not strong enough. It is better to respond One No-Trump as Three No-Trumps is your most likely game.

(E) ♠ Q3	(F) ♠ 4
♡ A2	♡ 2
◇ KQ10854	◇ KQJ1054
♣ 872	♣ AJ1043

Hand (E) is just right for a Two Diamond response. You will be happy whatever partner does next. With Hand (F) bid Two Diamonds, intending to bid clubs next time.

Lesson 102
Putting it into practice

As South, at Love All, you pick up:

♠ J432
♡ AJ2
◇ 1053
♣ AJ7

You hear your LHO open One Club and your partner overcalls One Diamond. Your RHO passes. What do you bid now?

If your partner had *opened* One Diamond you would have responded One Spade. Here it is different. North's overcall could be on as few as 8 or 9 HCP and you must make the bid that describes your hand best: an immediate One No-Trump. This ends the auction. West leads the king of clubs and you can see:

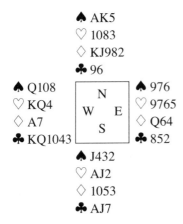

                    ♠ AK5
                    ♡ 1083
                    ◇ KJ982
                    ♣ 96
♠ Q108   N   ♠ 976
♡ KQ4   W   E   ♡ 9765
◇ A7   S   ◇ Q64
♣ KQ1043   ♣ 852
                    ♠ J432
                    ♡ AJ2
                    ◇ 1053
                    ♣ AJ7

Contract: One No-Trump by South
Lead: king of clubs

This deal is rather tricky, so you may find it easier to follow if you deal the hand out.

The first thing to do is duck the king of clubs lead. When you duck from AJx you force West either to give you a second trick in the suit, or to switch, which, in this instance, must also be beneficial for you.

West switches to the king of hearts which you win with the ace. Your next play must be to set about the diamond suit. If you play diamonds in such a way that you lose the first trick in the suit to *East*, he will play a club and the defenders will establish their tricks in that suit. Then when West gets the lead with a diamond he will have clubs to cash as well as the queen of hearts: four clubs, one heart and two diamonds – seven in all. So it is important that if you are to lose two diamond tricks you lose the first to *West*.

If West has both diamond honours you cannot fail; if East has both diamond honours you cannot succeed. The relevant situations are when the diamond honours are divided; you must decide who is more likely to have which diamond honour. You are missing 18 HCP. If East had the ace of diamonds, then West would have had 14 HCP and might have opened One No-Trump and not One Club.

Win the ace of hearts and play a diamond to the *king* and a diamond back to your ten and West's ace. He has no good defence and you will probably end up with eight tricks.

111

Lesson 103
The continuing auction

So, you have made your overcall, partner has made his response. What happens next?

After partner has raised the suit you overcalled

At the bottom end, a simple raise after an overcall is similar in strength to a raise after an opening bid but may be a little stronger. Because the overcall promises a five-card suit, a raise will usually contain only three-card support rather than the four you would expect for a raise after an opening bid. In order to think in terms of game, you need good opening-bid values in terms of high-card strength with some decent distribution thrown in. Consider the following hands after the bidding 1♡ – 1♠ – Pass – 2♠ – Pass:

(A)♠ AQJ94	(B)♠ AQ873
♡ A65	♡ 7
♢ 73	♢ K963
♣ K107	♣ AJ6

With Hand (A) you should pass. Despite your 14 HCP, your distribution is not good enough to warrant a game-try. Hand (B), on the other hand, is worth a try because you have good distribution as well as a maximum in terms of high cards. Bid your second suit, Three Diamonds. If partner has some high cards in diamonds he knows they are of greater use and can bid game.

This Three Diamond bid is known as a *long-suit game try*. It can also be used in an uninterrupted auction, say after 1♠ – Pass – 2♠ – Pass. It shows length in diamonds. Partner should press on to game either if he is maximum or if he has a ogod holding in diamonds. A good holding would be Q-J-x, K-x or even x-x; the worst holding is x-x-x.

After partner has responded One No-Trump or a new suit

Here partner does not have a fit for you but does promise more in the way of high cards. You can simply evaluate the high-card strength of the two hands. Look at the following hands after RHO has opened One Heart and you have overcalled One Spade.

(C)♠ AQJ94	(D)♠ AQ873
♡ KJ5	♡ 72
♢ 73	♢ K96
♣ J107	♣ AJ6

With Hand (C) if partner responds One No-Trump, pass. His range is 9–12 so you can't have the 25 HCP you need for game. If he bid Two Clubs or Two Diamonds, though, you can proceed with Two No-Trumps, showing an above-minimum overcall with good heart stoppers. With Hand (D), if partner bids One No-Trump, raise him to Two. If he has 11 or 12 points he will bid game. If he responds Two Clubs or Two Diamonds, raise him to Three to show extra values with a fit.

Lesson 104
A One No-Trump overcall

Sometimes, after your RHO has opened the bidding with One of suit, you find yourself looking at a balanced hand with a whole picture gallery of honour cards. We have seen that to overcall you need at least a five-card suit, so what is the solution? If you are strong enough you can overcall One No-Trump.

When we considered opening the bidding we agreed on a no-trump range of 12–14 HCP (though we did say at the time that there were other common agreements). But when your RHO has opened, the situation is different. To start with, it is less likely that your partner has very much, and secondly, if your LHO has 10 or more HCP he knows his side have comfortably more than half the points in the pack and will surely make a penalty double and punish you.

No, when your RHO has opened the bidding it is much more sensible to play a strong no-trump overcall, say a good 15 to a poor 18 HCP (i.e. the 15-count should have some extra playing strength or several tens, and the 18 count shouldn't).

Here are some examples of sound One No-Trump overcalls after your RHO opens One Heart.

(A)♠ K104
　♡ KQ6
　♢ AQ1076
　♣ J7

(B)♠ KJ102
　♡ A106
　♢ K973
　♣ AQ

Hand (A) is a minimum in terms of high-card points but has extra playing strength because of the diamond suit. Hand (B) is really a maximum: there are 17 HCP, the spade suit may be a good source of tricks, and a 4-4-3-2 distribution tends to generate more tricks than 4-3-3-3.

If partner overcalls One No-Trump, the subsequent bidding is exactly as if he had opened One No-Trump. We hope you can remember what that is; if not, refer back to Lessons 30 and 31. If your LHO opened One Heart and your partner overcalled One No-Trump, what would you bid with the following hands:

(C)♠ QJ1076
　♡ 865
　♢ 52
　♣ J72

(D)♠ Q742
　♡ Q4
　♢ A653
　♣ 1032

On Hand (C) bid Two Spades, a weakness take-out. Partner should always pass. On Hand (D), with 8 HCP, invite partner to bid game by raising him to Two No-Trumps. Partner will go on to Three with 17 or 18, but will pass with a weaker hand.

Lesson 105
Jump overcalls

A *jump overcall* is an overcall that is made at one level higher than is strictly necessary. The strength needed is a matter of partnership agreement. As usual we will recommend the middle-of-the-road course and suggest that you play them to be *intermediate*. This means that a jump overcall shows a minimum opening bid with a goodish six-card suit; occasionally you may make the bid with a seven-card suit, particularly at the three level.

Whatever suit is opened in front of you (though, of course, not your longest one – an overcall in the suit opened means something completely different), these hands are perfect intermediate jump overcalls.

(A) ♠ KQJ1065   (B) ♠ 7
   ♡ 6   ♡ AKJ1054
   ◇ A54   ◇ Q76
   ♣ 1076   ♣ K76

With Hand (A) bid Two Spades after an opening bid of One Club, One Diamond or One Heart. With Hand (B), bid Two Hearts over One Club or One Diamond, or Three Hearts over One Spade.

The following are not:

(C) ♠ J98653   (D) ♠ 7
   ♡ A4   ♡ AKJ1054
   ◇ A54   ◇ AJ7
   ♣ K5   ♣ K76

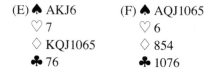

(E) ♠ AKJ6   (F) ♠ AQJ1065
   ♡ 7   ♡ 6
   ◇ KQJ1065   ◇ 854
   ♣ 76   ♣ 1076

On Hand (C) the suit is not strong enough. Start with a One Spade overcall whether your RHO opens One Club, One Diamond or One Heart. Although your suit is weak and you do not wish to encourage partner to lead it, the chances of your side being able to make a spade contract are too great for you to pass.

Hand (D) is too strong. How you deal with this hand-type is something we will cover later (see Lesson 111).

The problem with Hand (E) is the four-card spade suit. If the opening bid is One Club or One Heart, a jump overcall in diamonds may make it hard to find the spade fit; if the opening bid is One Spade, partner may find it hard to envisage Three No-Trumps when that is the best final contract. Start with a simple overcall in diamonds.

Hand (F) is too weak. Settle for One Spade.

A jump overcall is such a well-defined bid that no particular response structure is needed. Your choices are to pass, to raise partner, to make a natural bid in no-trumps or to bid a good new suit of your own, which is forcing for one round.

Lesson 106
Putting it into practice

No-one vulnerable. Dealer East.

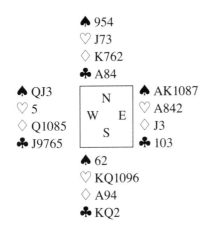

♠ 954
♡ J73
◇ K762
♣ A84

♠ QJ3
♡ 5
◇ Q1085
♣ J9765

N
W E
S

♠ AK1087
♡ A842
◇ J3
♣ 103

♠ 62
♡ KQ1096
◇ A94
♣ KQ2

South	West	North	East
–	–	–	1♠
2♡	2♠	3♡	All Pass

Contract: Three Hearts by South
Lead: queen of spades, followed by the jack
of spades and a third spade to East's king

The bidding on this hand was straightforward. After East opened One Spade, the South hand was worth a Two Heart overcall – although it is normally desirable to have a six-card suit for a two-level overcall, it is also important to get into the bidding when you have a good five-card major. After West's raise to Two Spades (which is more often only three-card support in a competitive auction), North was well worth a raise to Three Hearts with his three-card trump support and ace and king outside.

Plan the play in Three Hearts after the defenders start with three rounds of spades.

At the table declarer ruffed the third spade and played trumps. Unfortunately for declarer, East was on excellent form: he ducked the first two hearts and won the third. He then played a fourth round of spades which knocked out South's remaining trump. Declarer now tried to cash his minor-suit winners but East ruffed the third round of clubs and cashed a spade.

Once again, declarer should have started by counting his tricks – four hearts, two diamonds and three clubs – and his losers – two spades, one heart and one diamond.

He should have considered what could go wrong: while there would be no problem if trumps broke 3-2, on a 4-1 break he was in danger of running out of trumps. The solution was to discard a diamond on the third spade instead of ruffing. This diamond was going to be one of his four losers in any event, so losing it early rather than later could not cost. The difference is that now if the defence persist with spades declarer can ruff in the dummy, preserving his trump length in hand.

This is quite a common type of position. It is often right to discard a certain loser rather than ruff in the long trump hand.

Lesson 107
The take-out double 1

We have written about overcalls – simple, jump and One No-Trump. So, if you have a five-card suit in the range 9–15, or a six-card suit in the range 10–14, or a balanced hand in the range 15–18, you now know what to do. But there are several hands on which you may want to bid that do not fall into any of those categories. Suppose you hold one of the following hands after a One Heart opening by your right-hand opponent:

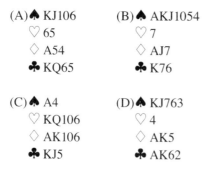

(A) ♠ KJ106
   ♡ 65
   ♢ A54
   ♣ KQ65

(B) ♠ AKJ1054
   ♡ 7
   ♢ AJ7
   ♣ K76

(C) ♠ A4
   ♡ KQ106
   ♢ AK106
   ♣ KJ5

(D) ♠ KJ763
   ♡ 4
   ♢ AK5
   ♣ AK62

Although you would like to make a bid on Hand (A) it doesn't fit into anything we have written about so far. We mentioned a while ago that Hand (B) was too strong for an intermediate jump overcall and that we would tell you later what to bid. Hand (C), with its 20 points, is too strong to overcall One No-Trump. Hand (D) looks too strong for a simple One Spade overcall.

Your solution is to make a *take-out double*. To double for penalties at the one level is almost always futile and wasteful;

with length in their suit you are happy and don't want to warn them of bad breaks. Nearly everyone plays that a double of an opening One of a suit is for take-out.

A double of an opening bid of One of a suit asks partner to choose between the other three suits. He must not pass this double unless he has considerable length and strength in the suit opened. To this end, it is important when you make a take-out double on a minimum hand that you have good support for all the suits other than the one opened. A 4-4-4-1 distribution with a singleton in the suit opened is ideal, but 4-4-3-2 or 5-4-3-1 are acceptable.

A take-out double may also be used to show a hand too strong to overcall. Hence it would be the first action with Hands (B), (C) and (D) above.

It is important to realise that the subsequent auction after a take-out double is unlike all the auctions we have looked at so far. In a normal auction, one partner shows some values and if the other partner has some values he makes a bid, then the first partner has a further chance to describe his hand, and so on. After a take-out double, the responder's bid is not *voluntary*. The double forced him to bid, so his response shows no values at all. If he does have some values he must make a special effort to tell his partner so. If he makes a minimum response, the original doubler needs significant extra values to bid on.

Lesson 108
The take-out double 2

The take-out double is an important weapon of competitive bidding and one which is often misunderstood by inexperienced players. It can be made on two different types of hand:

(1) Minimum hands of, say, 12–16 points where the intention is to pass partner's simple response. Obviously if partner makes a response that shows positive values then the doubler may bid again.

(2) Hands which are too strong for a simple, jump or One No-Trump overcall. Here the doubler's intention is to bid again whatever partner's response.

In this lesson we will be concerned only with the first hand-type. Consider the following hands after an opening bid of One Heart:

(A) ♠ KJ65   (B) ♠ J876
    ♡ 7   ♡ AK4
    ♢ A763   ♢ Q65
    ♣ KQ43   ♣ K76

(C) ♠ QJ52   (D) ♠ AQ4
    ♡ 3   ♡ 76
    ♢ AK1063 ♢ K1083
    ♣ KJ5   ♣ A972

Hand (A) is as near perfect a take-out double as you are ever likely to see. Hand (B) is too balanced, with too many high cards in hearts. Just because a hand is too weak for a One No-Trump overcall is no reason to double. You should pass instead. Hand (C) is a good take-out double. It is a much better alternative than a Two Diamond overcall with only a five-card suit. On Hand (D) double is fine, although some people may tell you you should have four spades for a take-out double of One Heart. In our view this is unnecessary, provided you have a good three-card holding and four cards in both minors.

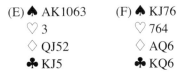

(E) ♠ AK1063   (F) ♠ KJ76
    ♡ 3   ♡ 764
    ♢ QJ52   ♢ AQ6
    ♣ KJ5   ♣ KQ6

Hand (E) is like Hand (C) but with the spades and diamonds swapped over. But here you have a perfectly respectable One Spade overcall, a better choice than a take-out double. Hand (F) is a little like Hand (B) but here we would double, although it could work out badly. Although the hand is balanced, it has a little extra strength and no high cards in hearts. We would pass if the four-card suit was in one of the minors. This is because partner's most likely response to a take-out double of One Heart is in spades. It is important that he should not be disappointed with your holding in that suit.

Lesson 109
Responding to a take-out double 1

When responding to partner's take-out double the most important thing to remember is that you have been *instructed* to bid by partner (Lesson 107). *You must bid even with no points at all.* Study these three hands carefully. If your LHO opened One Spade, partner doubled and the next hand passed, what would you bid with:

(A) ♠ 9865
♡ Q7
◇ QJ7
♣ 8732

(B) ♠ 7654
♡ 862
◇ 652
♣ 764

(C) ♠ QJ10976
♡ 3
◇ 872
♣ Q64

(D) ♠ KJ972
♡ 7
◇ QJ102
♣ Q62

Hand (A) is a fairly normal weak responding hand. Bid Two Clubs, your four-card suit. Hand (B) is everyone's nightmare. With no four-card suit to bid, you just have to bid your lowest three-card minor – here Two Clubs. Hand (C) is an example of the one sort of hand you may pass on. You can hope to make four trump tricks and so need only three top tricks from partner to beat One Spade doubled. Naturally, if your RHO bids something and you hold any of these three hands, you will pass gratefully.

With Hand (D) your suit is not strong enough to pass. Bid One No-Trump. Don't worry about holding a singleton heart – partner should have values in that suit.

Of course, you don't always have a poor hand. What do you think the right bid is on the following hands after your LHO has opened One Heart, partner has doubled and the next hand has passed?

(E) ♠ 86
♡ 762
◇ KJ54
♣ Q972

(F) ♠ Q2
♡ KJ105
◇ Q76
♣ J873

On Hand (E) you have a few values but not enough to do anything exciting. Which suit should you bid? The rule is that with two suits in response to a take-out double your first choice is to bid your longer; if they are the same length choose a major if you have one, otherwise choose the higher-ranking. You choose a major because, as in just about all aspects of bidding, one of your first aims is to find a major-suit fit. To make game in a major you need a trick fewer than you do in a minor, so explore that option first. You choose the higher because it leaves you with a more comfortable second bid should you wish to bid again. With Hand (E) bid Two Diamonds.

Hand (F) is a good example of a One No-Trump response, which shows 6–9 points with a good stopper in the opponents' suit.

Lesson 110
Responding to a take-out double 2

Of course, when partner makes a take-out double and you have some values you must do something to tell him so. Suppose your LHO opens One Heart, your partner doubles and your RHO passes. What do you bid with:

(A) ♠ KJ1053　　(B) ♠ KJ106
　　♡ 8743　　　　　♡ A76
　　♢ A5　　　　　　♢ Q872
　　♣ 73　　　　　　♣ 73

With Hand (A) jump to Two Spades. This shows about 7–9 points with a five-card spade suit, or a little more with only a four-card suit. Hand (B) is also a Two Spade bid. Don't worry about jumping in a chunky four-card suit, as partner has promised support for all the other suits (or else a strong hand that is going to bid again in any event).

Let's try some more hands. This time the bidding has gone: 1♠ – Double – Pass – ?

(C) ♠ 4　　　　　(D) ♠ 8743
　　♡ 9863　　　　　♡ KQ10542
　　♢ KQ10653　　　♢ A5
　　♣ K6　　　　　　♣ 5

On Hand (C), jump to Three Diamonds. When partner hears of your values he may be able to bid Three No-Trumps, in which case your long diamond suit will provide him with a lot of tricks.

With Hand (D) you must bid Four Hearts. Although you have only 9 HCP you have tremendous playing strength and are much too strong for Three Hearts. Try dealing out some 1-4-4-4 distribution hands with as few as 10 HCP. You will find you can make game facing most of them.

These two are a little harder. Again the bidding has gone: 1♠ – Double – Pass – ?

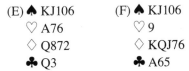

(E) ♠ KJ106　　(F) ♠ KJ106
　　♡ A76　　　　　♡ 9
　　♢ Q872　　　　♢ KQJ76
　　♣ Q3　　　　　♣ A65

Although in the last lesson we said that a One No-Trump response to a double showed positive values, Hand (E) is too strong. One No-Trump shows about 8–10 and Two No-Trumps shows 11–12, which is what you should bid here.

Hand (F) is very tricky. You are too strong to bid Three Diamonds which is what you bid with Hand (C) above. You could bid Four Diamonds or Five Diamonds but that would take you past your most likely game, which is Three No-Trumps. Remember that partner has promised support for all the other suits, so do not worry about your singleton heart – partner will have values there. With your good diamond suit, 14 HCP and double spade stopper go straight to Three No-Trumps yourself.

Lesson 111
The continuing auction

The first, and most frequent, hand-type for a take-out double is the sort we have already looked at where you want to find out your partner's best suit. The second hand-type is a hand too good to bid a simple, jump or One No-Trump overcall. If this is your hand you must tell partner about it on the next round.

Consider the following hands after the auction:

South	West	North	East
1♡	Dble	Pass	1♠
Pass	?		

(A) ♠ KQ4
   ♡ 76
   ◇ AKJ1065
   ♣ K3

(B) ♠ K5
   ♡ AQ106
   ◇ AK65
   ♣ A105

(C) ♠ KQJ4
   ♡ A4
   ◇ A1065
   ♣ Q72

(D) ♠ AK3
   ♡ 7
   ◇ AQ4
   ♣ KQJ1074

With Hand (A) you started with a take-out double because you were too strong for either a simple overcall of Two Diamonds or a jump overcall of Three Diamonds. There is no need to do anything dramatic here, a simple Two Diamonds describes your hand well. Partner should bid on with 5 or 6 HCP. Hand (B) was too strong for a One No-Trump overcall. You

started with a double because you were intending to rebid One No-Trump, so proceed with your plan and do so now. On Hand (C) you have extra values and can tell partner so by raising him to Two Spades. If you had a weaker hand you would simply pass One Spade, because partner may have very little. Hand (D) is even stronger than Hand (A). Jump to Three Clubs to tell partner so.

Now let's look at it from partner's point of view:

South	West	North	East
1♡	Dble	Pass	1♠
Pass	2◇	Pass	?

(E) ♠ KJ76
   ♡ 8532
   ◇ Q73
   ♣ 62

(F) ♠ A10986
   ♡ 853
   ◇ Q3
   ♣ 864

On Hand (E), with 6 HCP, including an honour in partner's suit, you must make another bid. Still, you don't have a heart stopper and eleven tricks is a lot to make. Content yourself with a simple raise to Three Diamonds and leave the rest to partner. Hand (F) has become much improved by partner's diamond bid but still Four Spades is the most likely game. Tell partner of your good spade suit and extra values by jumping to Three Spades. If he holds Hand (A) above he will bid on to the good game.

Lesson 112
Putting it into practice

It is time for some cardplay again. Remember to set out the cards and play through the hand as you read. And make sure you understand the rather aggressive bidding.

Both vulnerable. Dealer West.

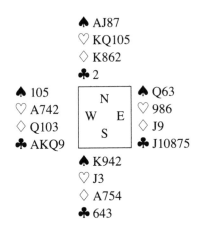

```
              ♠ AJ87
              ♡ KQ105
              ◇ K862
              ♣ 2
♠ 105                      ♠ Q63
♡ A742      N             ♡ 986
◇ Q103    W   E          ◇ J9
♣ AKQ9      S            ♣ J10875
              ♠ K942
              ♡ J3
              ◇ A754
              ♣ 643
```

South	West	North	East
–	1♣	Dble	Pass
2♠	Pass	4♠	All Pass

Contract: Four Spades by South
Lead: ace of clubs, following by the king of clubs

North-South's bidding was well judged. South was too strong for a simple One Spade response, so Two Spades was the right choice. Although North had only 13 HCP, his 4-4-4-1 distribution, along with his chunky heart suit persuaded him to overbid and he jumped optimistically to Four Spades.

West led a top club and continued with a second top club at trick two. Declarer ruffed in dummy, crossed to the king of spades and played a spade to dummy's jack. East won with the queen and returned a third spade, removing dummy's last trump. When West came in with the ace of hearts he cashed a club and declarer had to go one down.

Can you see how declarer could have done better?

Although he was a little unlucky, he could have more or less guaranteed his contract on any 3-2 spade break, whoever had the queen of spades. The correct line is to ruff the second club and play a heart to the jack at trick three. West wins the ace and perhaps returns a heart. Declarer wins the king of hearts, plays a trump to his king and a trump to dummy's ace. Now he cashes the queen and ten of hearts discarding two diamonds from hand. Declarer then plays a diamond to his ace, ruffs his last club in dummy, cashes the king of diamonds and ruffs his last diamond in hand. East can make his trump trick whenever he chooses but that is the third defensive trick and there is no chance for them to make any more.

Did you remember to deal out the hand and play it through?

Lesson 113
The opponents' take-out double 1

Now it is time to consider how to bid if the opponents make a take-out double against you.

Suppose your partner opens One Heart and the next hand doubles. What do you bid with the following hands?

(A) ♠ J65
  ♡ 5
  ♢ QJ105
  ♣ Q7432

(B) ♠ J976
  ♡ Q6
  ♢ KJ106
  ♣ Q76

The solution on Hand (A) is to pass. Had your RHO passed you would have bid One No-Trump, just in case your partner had a really strong hand. But here the situation is different; if he has a really strong hand he can bid again even if you pass. With Hand (B) you would have bid One Spade without the double, but now it is better to tell partner the general nature of your hand and bid One No-Trump. Your RHO probably has four spades for his double, so it is unlikely you have a fit in that suit.

(C) ♠ 42
  ♡ KJ5
  ♢ Q7542
  ♣ Q62

(D) ♠ KJ1072
  ♡ 63
  ♢ A54
  ♣ 982

With Hand (C) you should bid Two Hearts, which some would recommend even without the double. On Hand (D), bid One

Spade. With a five-card major, bid just as you would have without the double.

When the opponents enter the auction, it is important to describe your hand as accurately as possible in one bid. The chances have increased that the opponents will bid more and take away your bidding space; if so, partner may have to guess whether or not to bid further. If you bid One No-Trump on Hand (A) partner may be encouraged to rebid a six-card heart suit; if you bid One Spade on Hand (B) partner may be tempted to raise you with only three spades; if you bid One No-Trump on Hand (C) partner will be discouraged from competing in hearts.

When the auction shows signs of becoming competitive it is important that you support partner as enthusiastically as possible. A raise to Two Hearts is often made with only three-card support; when you have four-card support you may jump to Three Hearts with fewer high cards than without the double. The following hands would both be suitable for the sequence: 1♡ – Double – 3♡:

(E) ♠ 765
  ♡ A532
  ♢ QJ65
  ♣ 82

(F) ♠ 8
  ♡ KJ106
  ♢ J10532
  ♣ 872

Lesson 114
The opponents' take-out double 2

In the last lesson we saw some examples of hands where you would raise partner's opening bid of One Heart to Three Hearts after an intervening double. What then do you bid with a full-blown normal Three Heart bid? The answer is that you use a special convention that is just about standard throughout the bridge world. It is known as the Truscott Two No-Trumps (after its inventor Alan Truscott, who emigrated from the UK to the USA many years ago and is now bridge correspondent of the *New York Times*). The idea is that the sequence: $1\heartsuit$ – Double – 2NT shows a hand that would have bid Three Hearts without the double. The following would both be good examples:

(A) ♠ A54
     ♡ KQ65
     ◇ Q6
     ♣ 9854

(B) ♠ KQ
    ♡ A7653
    ◇ 762
    ♣ J65

Other than the exceptions discussed in the last couple of articles, you generally bid in the same way after the opponents have made a take-out double as without it. But there is a new bid at your disposal: a *redouble*. To redouble you need at least 10 HCP and either a wish to penalise the opponents or a hand that is awkward to bid any other way. The following hands would be suitable for a redouble after $1\heartsuit$ – Double:

(C) ♠ AJ103
    ♡ 4
    ◇ QJ106
    ♣ K982

(D) ♠ A76
    ♡ KJ6
    ◇ Q10965
    ♣ 72

(E) ♠ AQ5
    ♡ 76
    ◇ K1095
    ♣ K874

(F) ♠ A74
    ♡ 73
    ◇ AQ1074
    ♣ K63

With Hand (C) you are happy to double the opponents in whatever suit they bid. On Hand (D) without the double you would have started with Two Diamonds and had a tricky decision if partner had rebid Two Hearts: should you raise to Three Hearts or not? This hand is not about your diamond suit; it is much more accurately described by starting with a redouble and bidding Two Hearts on the next round, showing 10–11 HCP with three-card heart support (never start with a redouble with four-card support; either raise directly or bid Two No-Trumps, as above). With Hand (E) you can't bid Two No-Trumps as that would show four-card heart support; redouble first, intending to bid Two No-Trumps next time. With Hand (F) start with a redouble; maybe partner can double them in a black suit, otherwise you can bid diamonds next time.

Lesson 115
The opponents overcall 1

Over the past few lessons we have seen how to bid if the opponents make a take-out double, but what if they overcall? Suppose you hold the following hands; your partner has opened One Heart and your right-hand opponent overcalled Two Clubs:

(A) ♠ A1064   (B) ♠ KJ1075
    ♡ Q43   ♡ Q4
    ♢ J1043   ♢ AQ5
    ♣ 54   ♣ 763

With Hand (A) you would have bid One Spade without the intervention. Unfortunately you cannot now bid Two Spades; that would show a five-card suit and at least the values for a 'two-over-one' response (i.e. the values needed for responding in a new suit at the two level after a one-level opening in a suit). Here you should bid Two Hearts. When the opponents get into the auction it is important to support your partner as quickly as possible. You only need three-card support once the opponents have intervened.

With Hand (B) you simply bid Two Spades. This shows a five-card suit and is forcing for one round.

Now try these:

(C) ♠ AQ2   (D) ♠ KQ3
    ♡ 6   ♡ Q62
    ♢ J1054   ♢ 10943
    ♣ KJ1065   ♣ KJ6

With Hand (C) you should double. This is a penalty double showing good clubs and a minimum of about 8 or 9 HCP. You cannot bid Three Clubs. This shows something completely different which we will look at in Part VII.

With Hand (D) bid Two No-Trumps, just as you would have done without the intervention, though now it is important that you hold at least one, and preferably two, club stoppers.

(E) ♠ A54   (F) ♠ A54
    ♡ Q543   ♡ Q543
    ♢ J763   ♢ AJ54
    ♣ 32   ♣ 32

If you only need three-card support to make a simple raise in a competitive auction, you should try as hard as possible to bid more when you have four-card support. In competition Hand (E) is just about worth Three Hearts. It may be vital for partner to know about your fourth trump. The more trumps you have between you, the more important it is for you to keep bidding in a competitive auction. If you are going to bid Three Hearts with Hand (E), then you clearly need to do more with Hand (F). If you have a nice crisp 11 points with good controls, take the plunge and bid all the way to game.

Lesson 116
The opponents overcall 2

This time put yourself in opener's seat:

> ♠ AQ43
> ♡ AK652
> ◇ 5
> ♣ A54

and the bidding goes 1♡ – 2◇ – Pass – Pass. What do you bid?

If you pass that is the end of it. You will defend Two Diamonds. If it goes down you will wish you had doubled it; if it makes maybe you could have made some contract your way. The solution is to double. This is another example of a take-out double. It suggests extra values, shortage in diamonds and support for all the other suits. Partner could have any of the following hands:

(A)	♠ KJ62	(B)	♠ 763
	♡ 42		♡ 5
	◇ 9832		◇ KJ754
	♣ 873		♣ 8732

(C)	♠ J54	(D)	♠ 952
	♡ 982		♡ 7
	◇ 8742		◇ J762
	♣ 763		♣ KQ1073

With Hand (A) he will bid Two Spades, a contract which should make at least eight tricks. On Hand (B) he did not have enough to double Two Diamonds himself but is delighted to opt for this by passing your double once you have shown extra values. On Hand (C) he will bid an unhappy Two Hearts, but this has good chances of making and if it doesn't, your opponents may have been able to make Two Diamonds. On Hand (D) he will bid Three Clubs on a hand that was not strong enough to bid the first time.

If you have a good hand with shortage in the opponents' suit, it is important to bid aggressively in a competitive auction. In particular, if you can double, it is a good idea to do so. If partner has values in the opponents' suit he can pass and you collect a penalty; if his values are elsewhere then you can hope to make a contract your way. Opener should double on the hand given at the beginning of this lesson even if his right-hand opponent had raised to Three Diamonds, i.e. after the auction: 1♡ – 2◇ – Pass – 3◇.

Of course, opener does not have to double. Suppose he has one of the following hands:

(E)	♠ A4	(F)	♠ AQ2
	♡ KQJ106		♡ KQJ1065
	◇ AQ3		◇ A43
	♣ QJ5		♣ 6

With Hand (E) he should bid Two No-Trumps and with Hand (F) Two Hearts. Although these bids are not without risk, they are unlikely to come to too much harm and passing can be risky as well.

Lesson 117
The competitive auction

To improve your competitive bidding you must consider the bidding first from one side's point of view and then from the other. First we looked at the requirements for a take-out double, then the responses to it. However, in the last few lessons we have looked at what to do when an opponent doubles or bids over partner's opening bid – it is important to support him as vigorously as possible. We now need to look at the other side of that coin.

In Lesson 110 we gave several examples of jump responses after a take-out double of One Heart. These were the hands:

(A)	♠ KJ1053	(B)	♠ KJ106
	♡ 8743		♡ A76
	◇ A5		◇ Q872
	♣ 73		♣ 73

Now, if the bidding had gone 1♡ – Dble – Pass you would have bid Two Spades with Hands (A) and (B). Now suppose it goes 1♡ – Dble – 3♡. Do you pass or bid your suit at a higher level?

There are several reasons why you should bid. One thing you will learn quickly when you start playing bridge against active opponents is that when they have a fit, you have a fit as well. Suppose they have a nine-card fit in hearts (likely on this auction). Then your side has only four cards in hearts. Since your side has 26 cards, it has 22 non-

hearts, and *it is 100% certain that your side will have at least an eight-card fit* (and most probably a nine-card fit). So, the greater their fit, the greater your fit. You can count when you hold Hand (A) that partner can have no more than a singleton heart; on Hand (B) he has at most a doubleton. So consider these possible hands which your partner might hold for his take-out double:

(C)	♠ A842	(D)	♠ A842
	♡ 5		♡ 94
	◇ KJ64		◇ KJ4
	♣ AJ62		♣ KJ62

The singleton heart and good controls in Hand (C) make it just worth a raise to Four Spades – an excellent contract facing Hand (A) though less good facing Hand (B). Hand (D) would pass Three Spades, a contract which has good chances facing (A) or (B).

If the opponents' bidding was even more vigorous, say 1♡ – Dble – 4♡, you should still bid. There are many hands partner could have on which he will pass Four Hearts when you can make game. Bid Four Spades on Hand (A) or (B) above.

Lesson 118
Putting it into practice

When you play in a suit contract rather than no-trumps, it will often be because you need your trumps for a specific purpose: ruffing the defenders' long suit, ruffing your own losers, setting up a long suit by ruffing, and so on. It is important to be the one who decides when trumps are drawn and to ensure you have more of them than either of the defenders.

No-one vulnerable. Dealer North.

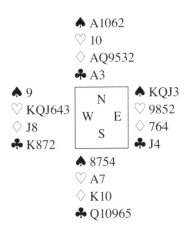

	♠ A1062	
	♡ 10	
	◊ AQ9532	
	♣ A3	

♠ 9	N	♠ KQJ3
♡ KQJ643	W E	♡ 9852
◊ J8	S	◊ 764
♣ K872		♣ J4

	♠ 8754	
	♡ A7	
	◊ K10	
	♣ Q10965	

South	West	North	East
–	1♡	Dble	2♡
2♠	Pass	4♠	All Pass

Contract: Four Spades by South
Lead: king of hearts

Although North had only 15 HCP it was a good hand and he decided to start with a double; if partner bid spades he could raise, otherwise he would bid his diamonds.

Usually, after an opponent makes a take-out double, four-card support and a few values is enough for a jump raise, but here East did not want to make it too difficult for his opponents to bid spades. Sure enough, over Two Hearts, South was able to bid Two Spades and North raised to Four.

Declarer won the ace of hearts and played ace and another trump, hoping the suit broke 3-2. Disaster. East drew all the rest of the trumps and the defenders then cashed five heart tricks. Five down.

A little more care would have seen declarer home. Suppose he wins the ace of hearts and plays a spade to West's nine and dummy's ten. What can East do? Suppose he wins his jack and plays a second heart. Declarer ruffs and cashes the ace of spades, finding out the bad news (note that had trumps broken 3-2 he would have been no worse a position than by playing ace and another). Now he sets about the diamonds. East can ruff in when he likes, and then draw dummy's last trump, but the ace of clubs is still in dummy as an entry for the diamonds. Declarer loses just three trump tricks.

By ducking the first round of spades, declarer kept trump control, a play that made five tricks difference to the eventual outcome.

Lesson 119
More on take-out doubles

Suppose you hold one of the following hands, but this time the bidding goes 1♡ – Pass – 2♡ and you are in the fourth seat:

(A) ♠ AQ42
♡ 5
◇ K654
♣ A862

(B) ♠ AQ42
♡ 94
◇ KJ4
♣ K1062

You should double on both these hands. Remember, when the opponents have a fit, so do you, and you may be able to make a partscore, or even a game, your way.

Sometimes your right-hand opponent changes the suit instead of supporting his partner. Suppose the bidding goes: 1◇ – Pass – 1♡ and you hold:

(C) ♠ 763
♡ KQJ107
◇ K52
♣ A3

(D) ♠ A104
♡ KQ107
◇ KJ4
♣ AJ7

A double after this sequence is for take-out, just as it would be directly over One Diamond, but here, because the opponents have bid two suits, your double shows just the other two, here spades and clubs. On Hand (C), with its length and strength in hearts, you must pass. Hand (D) is strong and balanced, so overcall One No-Trump, as you would have done in second seat.

(E) ♠ AQ52
♡ 873
◇ A3
♣ KQ105

(F) ♠ KJ1062
♡ 5
◇ 76
♣ AQ843

(G) ♠ AQ42
♡ 6
◇ A53
♣ KQ1054

(H) ♠ KQ1054
♡ 6
◇ A53
♣ AQ42

Although you do not need more than four cards in each of the two unbid suits to make a take-out double, it is safer to have a little more distribution. On the first sequence (1♡ – Pass – 2♡), your opponents have a fit, so you also have a fit, making it relatively safe for you to enter the auction. After 1◇ – Pass – 1♡, they have not established a fit, so it is more dangerous.

Hand (E) is a reasonable take-out double even after the second sequence, because of the extra values. If partner's values are in the red suits, he can bid One No-Trump. Hands (F) and (G) are both good take-out doubles after 1◇ – Pass – 1♡. Even though Hand (F) has only 10 HCP, the 5-5 distribution makes it a powerful hand. With Hand (H), where your only five-card suit is a major, it is better to bid One Spade. Because spades are the higher ranking suit, it is much more likely that you want to compete in spades than in clubs, and a double may make it hard for partner to compete with only three-card spade support.

Lesson 120
A double of One No-Trump

You should now be confident that a double of an opening bid of One of a suit shows, in the first instance, shortage in that suit, support for the other three suits and about opening values. What then is the meaning of a double of a One No-Trump opening?

Since the opponents have not bid a suit, it cannot be a take-out double. It is generally played as showing a strong balanced hand. Although doubles of strong no-trumps can turn out quite well, it is more frequently used against the weak (12–14) no-trump. The double should show 16+ HCP, or perhaps a little less when the hand has a good suit to lead. Here are some examples:

(A) ♠ KJ105　　(B) ♠ KQJ1087
　　♡ AQ5　　　　♡ A76
　　◇ J106　　　　◇ AK
　　♣ AQ6　　　　♣ K5

Hands (A) and (B) are good doubles of One No-Trump. Hand (A) has 17 HCP but no really attractive lead. It is probably best to start with the jack of diamonds, hoping to give nothing away. With Hand (B) you have an excellent opening lead and can guarantee eight tricks in defence against One No-Trump.

If your partner doubles One No-Trump you should nearly always pass. He knows you have very little and will not thank you for bidding. The only time you should remove the double is with a very weak hand and a long (at least five cards) suit.

Very often when someone doubles One No-Trump, the next hand removes to Two of a suit. It is important when that happens that the partner of the original doubler bids when he has some values, for the doubler has shown most of his values and will not bid again when he has a hand such as (A) above – though he would bid Two Spades with Hand (B) whatever happened.

Consider the following hands after the sequence: 1NT – Dble – 2♣ – ?

(C) ♠ Q64　　(D) ♠ A9762
　　♡ J76　　　　♡ J43
　　◇ 752　　　　◇ Q74
　　♣ KJ95　　　♣ 52

With Hand (C), double. If partner's hand is balanced you should collect a nice penalty. With Hand (D), bid Two Spades. This shows about 5–8 HCP and a five-card suit. The rest is up to partner. If he has Hand (A) above he will raise to Three Spades with his four-card support and you can decide whether or not to press on to the pushy game.

Lesson 121
Putting it into practice

There is no great point to the play and defence of this hand though we do recommend that you deal it out and follow the play. We have included it simply to show you the pleasure that can be gained from taking a good penalty from a low-level contract. You are West; your hand should look familiar as it appeared in the previous lesson.

Both vulnerable. Dealer North.

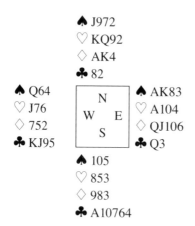

```
              ♠ J972
              ♡ KQ92
              ◇ AK4
              ♣ 82
  ♠ Q64      ┌─────┐     ♠ AK83
  ♡ J76      │  N  │     ♡ A104
  ◇ 752      │W   E│     ◇ QJ106
  ♣ KJ95     │  S  │     ♣ Q3
             └─────┘
              ♠ 105
              ♡ 853
              ◇ 983
              ♣ A10764
```

South	West	North	East
–	–	1NT	Dble
2♣	Dble	All Pass	

Contract: Two Clubs doubled, by South
Lead: five of diamonds

Remember, East's double of One No-Trump did not ask West to bid. A double of an opening of One of a *Suit* asks you to bid, but this was a penalty double, showing 16 or so HCP in a balanced hand (if his hand is not balanced partner will let you know later). You should pass this double unless you are very weak with a long suit.

When South bids Two Clubs you are correct to double. If your partner has 16 HCP in a balanced hand, your opponents have only 17 between them and a 5-2 fit.

You had a tricky opening lead to find. It is usually a good idea in this type of auction where you know your partner has strength to try to make a safe lead. The five of diamonds (MUD) was a good choice.

Declarer wins your diamond lead with his ace and there is very little he can do. Perhaps his best shot is to try a spade, hoping to establish a trick there on which to discard one of his red-suit losers. So he plays a spade to his ten and your queen (your partner should not go in with one of his honours as he can see that that will eventually establish a spade trick for declarer in the dummy). You play another diamond. Declarer wins the king, plays a club to his ace and a spade to dummy's seven and your partner's eight. You can more or less defend how you like now, for you must always take two spades, two hearts, one diamond and three clubs, making eight tricks in all; declarer goes three down for an 800 penalty.

Lesson 122
Protective bidding

When the opponents' bidding dies at a low level and you are in the pass-out seat (e.g. after 1♡ – Pass – Pass) with, say, 9 HCP, you should realise that partner probably has opening bid values or thereabouts – perhaps his suit is hearts or he has a balanced hand with 10–14 points. You should bid if you possibly can, and not let your opponents play quietly at a safe level. In the following bidding problems you are South:

West	North	East	South	
1♡	Pass	Pass	?	♠ K765
				♡ 8
				◇ KJ65
				♣ Q1065

Double. Although you have only 9 HCP, it would be cowardly to allow your opponents to play in One Heart. Partner probably has 12 or 13 HCP but was not strong enough to overcall One No-Trump. He should make allowances for you being up to a king weaker in fourth seat than you would be in second position.

West	North	East	South	
1♡	Pass	Pass	?	♠ K54
				♡ AQ4
				◇ J1076
				♣ Q106

Bid **One No-Trump**. Although you would not be strong enough for this action in second seat, in the *protective* position it is a different matter. Partner must have some values or East would not have passed his partner's opening bid. A One No-Trump overcall in the protective position shows about 12–15 HCP.

West	North	East	South	
–	–	1♡	Pass	♠ K765
2♡	Pass	Pass	?	♡ 8
				◇ KJ65
				♣ Q1065

Double. You were not strong enough for a take-out double on the first round but now it is safe for you to double: (a) partner heard you pass earlier so will not overestimate your values; (b) now you know your opponents have a fit, so you must have one too. Maybe you can make a partscore, or maybe your opponents will bid Three Hearts and go one down.

West	North	East	South	
–	–	1♡	Pass	♠ K765
2♡	Pass	Pass	?	♡ 865
				◇ AQ5
				♣ A76

Double. On this hand it was your distribution that was unsuitable for a first-round double, but it is safer now. Most of the time partner will be able to bid either a four-card spade suit or he will have a five-card minor, because he is probably short in hearts.

Lesson 123
Putting it into practice

There are several points of interest in the bidding and play of this hand.

East-West vulnerable. Dealer West.

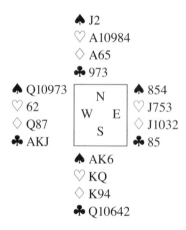

```
                ♠ J2
                ♡ A10984
                ◇ A65
                ♣ 973
    ♠ Q10973   ┌─────┐   ♠ 854
    ♡ 62       │  N  │   ♡ J753
    ◇ Q87      │W   E│   ◇ J1032
    ♣ AKJ      │  S  │   ♣ 85
               └─────┘
                ♠ AK6
                ♡ KQ
                ◇ K94
                ♣ Q10642
```

South	West	North	East
–	1♠	Pass	Pass
Dble	Pass	2♡	Pass
2NT	Pass	3NT	All Pass

Contract: Three No-Trumps by South
Lead: seven of spades

South's hand is too strong to overcall One No-Trump overcall in the *protective* position (that would have been the right call had *East* opened One Spade). A One No-Trump overcall in the protective position shows 12–15 HCP. So, South doubles, intending to rebid no-trumps on the next round.

North's correct action is also different from what it would have been had South doubled in the direct position. In that instance, North's correct bid, with 9 HCP and a good five-card suit, would have been Three Hearts. However, in the protective position South might be much weaker than he ever would be in second seat and North should be more restrained. Here he should bid Two Hearts and let South bid again if he has extra values.

That is what South does and the excellent game is reached.

At trick one you play the jack of spades from dummy and it holds the trick. Cover up the East and West hands and plan the play.

You could cash the king and queen of hearts, cross to the ace of diamonds and hope the hearts came in, in which case you would have ten tricks. But what if they don't?

There is a way to ensure nine tricks however the hearts break. Win the jack of spades, play a heart to your king and then play the queen of hearts and overtake it with dummy's ace. If the jack has not fallen, continue with the ten of hearts. East can win his jack whenever he pleases, but you can cross back to the ace of diamonds for the rest of your heart winners.

As usual, counting tricks is the key. If hearts break you have ten tricks, so you can afford to lose a heart trick.

Lesson 124
Competitive bidding quiz 1

What would you bid after the following auctions, holding the hands given:

(1)

West	North	East	South	♠ 87
1♡	1NT	Pass	?	♡ 853
				◇ KQ9765
				♣ A4

(2)

West	North	East	South	♠ 87
1♡	Dble	Pass	?	♡ 853
				◇ KQ9765
				♣ A4

(3)

West	North	East	South	♠ 87
1♡	Dble	2♡	?	♡ 853
				◇ KQ9765
				♣ A4

(4)

West	North	East	South	♠ 87
1♡	1♠	Pass	?	♡ 853
				◇ KQ9765
				♣ A4

(1) **Bid Three No-Trumps**. Partner has shown 15–18 HCP so you should have enough for game with your good source of diamond tricks, along with an outside entry. You would not jump in diamonds in this position unless you were looking for a contract other than Three No-Trumps.

(2) **Bid Three Diamonds**. This time partner has not shown any interest in playing in no-trumps, so you must show your diamonds. You would bid Two Diamonds with no values at all, so you must jump to show partner you have real interest in game.

(3) **Bid Four Diamonds**. When East supports hearts your hand improves because you now know partner will have at most a doubleton in the suit. To bid Three Diamonds would not do your hand justice – that is what you would bid without the ace of clubs. To show serious game interest you need to jump. Don't worry about going past Three No-Trumps; your side probably doesn't have a heart stopper in any event.

(4) **Two Diamonds**. Partner has only made an overcall but he could have quite a strong hand. When you change the suit you show a few values, say at least 9 or 10 points. If partner is minimum he will usually pass, but if he is maximum or has a good fit for diamonds he may bid on.

Lesson 125
Competitive bidding quiz 2

Which West hand fits the given auction best?

(1)
South	West	North	East
1♡	1♠	Pass	2♣
Pass	3♣		

(A)♠ AK762   (B)♠ AK762
    ♡ 65   ♡ 4
    ♢ Q54   ♢ 763
    ♣ A87   ♣ AQJ7

Answer: **Hand (A)**. Hand (B) is too strong. With such a good hand you should bid Four Clubs, which is a strong game invitation.

(2)
South	West	North	East
1♡	1♠	Pass	1NT
Pass	3♣		

(C)♠ AKJ105   (D)♠ AKJ105
    ♡ 6   ♡ 62
    ♢ 87   ♢ K7
    ♣ AQ1094 ♣ A1094

Answer: **Hand (C)**. Three Clubs shows a strong distributional hand. Hand (D) is too balanced to suggest looking for a minor-suit game. Just bid Three No-Trumps. Although you may have only 23 points between the two hands, that is often enough for Three No-Trumps when you know that all the opponents' high cards are in one hand.

(3)
South	West	North	East
–	–	1♡	Dble
Pass	2♣	Pass	2♠
Pass	4♠		

(E)♠ K104   (F)♠ K104
   ♡ 8732   ♡ 8732
   ♢ 4   ♢ 4
   ♣ KJ762   ♣ AK763

Answer: **Hand (E)**. Hand (F) is too strong for an original Two Club bid; you should have bid Three Clubs.

(4)
South	West	North	East
–	–	–	1♡
Dble	Rdble	1♠	Pass
Pass	2♡		

(G)♠ 76   (H)♠ 764
   ♡ AQ64   ♡ AQ6
   ♢ 763   ♢ 7632
   ♣ KQ105   ♣ KQ5

Answer: **Hand (H)** would be a perfect West hand. With four-card support, as in Hand (G), you should never start with a redouble. You should have bid Two No-Trumps on the first round. If you do not understand this, refer back to Lesson 114. Two No-Trumps after your opponent has made a take-out double shows a good raise to Three of the suit opened.

Part VI
Strong Hands

All of us like picking up good hands and one of the most exciting things you can do in the game of bridge is bid and make a slam. It is important to make the most of your strong hands and the lessons in this section should help you do just that.

Lesson 126
Two of a suit

In Part II we said that you needed about 6 HCP to respond to partner's opening bid in a suit. So what do you do if you have a strong opening hand, where you can see that game might make even if partner has fewer than 6 HCP?

Different parts of the world have come up with different answers to this problem but in this country we traditionally use the 'Acol Two' to show a strong hand (though a Two Club opening shows something slightly different and we will not consider that for another few lessons).*

An Acol Two bid shows a hand of power and quality with at least eight tricks. The opening bid itself is forcing for one round. Below are a few examples:

(A) ♠ AKQ1076   (B) ♠ none
    ♡ AJ4   ♡ KQJ652
    ◇ 7   ◇ AJ53
    ♣ KQ4   ♣ AK2

Open Two Spades on Hand (A) and Two Hearts on Hand (B).

The hand does not have to be single-suited:

(C) ♠ KQJ95   (D) ♠ AQ762
    ♡ AKJ103   ♡ none
    ◇ A5   ◇ AKQJ105
    ♣ 7   ♣ K2

Open Two Spades on Hand (C) and Two Diamonds on Hand (D).

Notice that on all these hands, only the tiniest amount of help from partner is needed to make game.

What about the following hands?

(E) ♠ AJ763   (F) ♠ AKQJ10652
    ♡ AK76   ♡ 65
    ◇ AK3   ◇ 3
    ♣ A   ♣ 102

Although Hand (E) is very strong in terms of points, it does not have the playing strength of the previous hands. It is too strong to open with a One-bid, but this is the type of hand you need for a Two Club opening, which we will deal with later.

Although Hand (F) has eight tricks, it does not have enough *defensive strength* (i.e. high cards outside the trump suit) for a Two-bid. On this hand, where all your points are in a very long suit, it is best to open Four Spades. Can you work out why? We will return to this subject later.

---

* In many parts of the world Two Clubs (sometimes Two Diamonds as well) is the only strong bid. Then an opening bid of Two of a major (sometimes Two Diamonds too) is weak, showing a six-card suit but less than opening values. Such an opening can make life very difficult for opponents. This method of playing is becoming more common in the UK nowadays.

Lesson 127
Responding to Two of a suit

In the previous lesson we said that an Acol Two-bid was *forcing for one round*. That means that the responder *cannot pass*. In order to differentiate between good and bad responding hands, a convention was developed whereby you make one response to show a weak hand while all other responses show some values. The response showing weakness is called a *negative* response. Traditionally Two No-Trumps was used as the negative but, although that is still widespread today, many modern players use the next suit up – called a Herbert negative.

In this course we aim to keep things simple and recommend the ordinary Two No-Trump negative. To make a positive response at the three level you generally need about what you would need to respond at the two level after One of a suit; if you can make your positive bid at the two level you do not need quite so many values.

Here are some responding hands after a Two Heart opening:

(A) ♠ AK543　　(B) ♠ K543
　　♡ 76　　　　　♡ 73
　　♢ J103　　　　♢ QJ3
　　♣ 873　　　　♣ Q432

Hand (A) is a clear Two Spade response. Aces and kings are particularly important when responding to partner's Two-bid. If your majors were swapped and partner had

opened Two Spades, it would be borderline whether or not to respond Three Hearts. Although Hand (B) has the same 8 HCP, it is a clear negative. After all, just because you make a negative does not mean you must stay out of game. When partner makes his rebid you can (and should on this hand) bid on to game.

What about when you have support for partner? Look at these hands after a Two Spade opening bid:

(C) ♠ J543　　(D) ♠ J543
　　♡ K3　　　　♡ Q3
　　♢ A762　　　♢ KQ43
　　♣ J32　　　　♣ J63

These two hands have the same distribution and the same number of HCP points. The difference lies in the number of controls (aces and kings). With Hand (C) a slam is quite likely – an excellent contract if partner has Hand (A) in Lesson 126. With Hand (D) there may well be three losers.

With Hand (C) respond Three Spades. This shows a hand with slam interest. It is forcing. With Hand (D) jump to Four Spades. This shows about 7–9 HCP with at least three-card trump support but it denies an ace or two kings. If you have a slightly weaker hand with support for partner you must bid as on Hand (B), i.e. start with a negative Two No-Trumps and then raise partner to game.

Lesson 128
Opening Two No-Trumps

All the way back in Lesson 32 we looked at bidding balanced hands that were too strong to open One No-Trump. If you have 15–17 you open in a suit and rebid One No-Trump; if you have 18–19 you open in a suit and make a jump rebid in no-trumps; but if you have 20–22 you must open Two No-Trumps.

The following hands would be suitable for a Two No-Trump opening:

(A) ♠ AQ3 (B) ♠ KQ654
  ♡ AJ5   ♡ AQ
  ◇ AJ104   ◇ KQ10
  ♣ KQ5   ♣ AJ5

Hand (A) is a completely balanced 21-count. Open Two No-Trumps. Hand (B) is tricky. Even though you have a five-card spade suit, you still have a balanced 21 HCP, so open Two No-Trumps. You are too strong for One Spade and, as we have seen, a Two Spade opening bid needs more playing strength.

There is no weakness take-out after a Two No-Trump opening. Although after a One No-Trump opening a simple bid in a suit shows a weak hand and is to play; after Two No-Trumps, a bid in a suit is forcing, asking partner to choose between game in that suit and Three No-Trumps.

Look at the following responding hands after partner opens Two No-Trumps:

(C) ♠ K642 (D) ♠ J732
  ♡ 1043   ♡ K9832
  ◇ Q5   ◇ J6
  ♣ 10642   ♣ 73

With Hand (C) raise directly to Three No-Trumps. Although you have only 5 HCP, partner's average is 21, which will give you the 26 you usually need. If you doubt this, put this hand opposite (A) and then deal out the remaining cards to the defenders. I think you will find that much more often than not declarer will succeed in his game.

With Hand (D) respond Three Hearts. If partner has four-card support he will always raise you to Four Hearts. Otherwise he will bid Three Spades if he has four or five spades. With no four-card major and a doubleton heart he will bid Three No-Trumps. With three-card support he should look at the rest of his hand. He should usually raise your suit when he has a doubleton but when he is 4-3-3-3, as Hand (A) above, he should prefer Three No-Trumps. Apart from anything else, it is harder for the defenders when the stronger hand is concealed.

Lesson 129
Putting it into practice

Back to the table and a lovely strong hand to bid and play.

Both vulnerable. Dealer South.

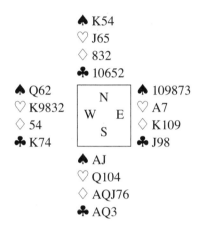

```
            ♠ K54
            ♡ J65
            ◇ 832
            ♣ 10652
♠ Q62       ┌─────┐    ♠ 109873
♡ K9832     │  N  │    ♡ A7
◇ 54        │W   E│    ◇ K109
♣ K74       │  S  │    ♣ J98
            └─────┘
            ♠ AJ
            ♡ Q104
            ◇ AQJ76
            ♣ AQ3
```

South	West	North	East
2NT	Pass	3NT	All Pass

Contract: Three No-Trumps by South
Lead: three of hearts

West's three of hearts lead went to East's ace and East returned the seven of hearts. On the first trick declarer had played the four and on the second trick, in an effort to force an entry with the jack of hearts, had played the queen. However, West let declarer's queen of hearts hold the second trick.

With only one entry to dummy and rather than pin everything on East having Kx of diamonds, declarer played ace and another diamond from his own hand. But East won the king and switched to a club. Declarer had no choice but to finesse and when that lost he was two down.

Do you see how he could have done better?

He was thinking along the right lines when he played the queen of hearts at trick two. He forced West to play well and duck that trick. Had he played the ten West would have won his king and returned the suit, still denying declarer his extra entry to dummy. However, declarer's thinking started a trick too late. What he should have done was play the queen of hearts under East's ace at trick one. Now when East returns the suit the defenders cannot prevent declarer reaching dummy in hearts. Declarer is in control, taking one diamond finesse when in dummy with the jack of hearts and another using the king of spades as entry. When East turns up with Kxx in diamonds the pushy game is made.

Lesson 130
The Two Club opening

We have seen some pretty good hands at the beginning of this section, but the *pièce de résistance* of the Acol system is the Two Club opener. This shows a seriously good hand, either 23–24 points in a balanced hand (shown by a Two No-Trump rebid) or any game-forcing hand (shown by any other rebid). It would be rare for the hand to contain fewer than 20 HCP and it will usually contain more. Here are some examples:

(A) ♠ AQ3
 ♡ KJ104
 ◇ AK32
 ♣ AQ

(B) ♠ AQJ65
 ♡ AK3
 ◇ K4
 ♣ KQJ

With both these two hands open Two Clubs and rebid Two No-Trumps showing 23–24 HCP. It would be a mistake to rebid Two Spades on Hand (B). Even though this hand is very powerful, it is not worth forcing to game facing a complete bust. It is a balanced hand so rebid Two No-Trumps. The sequence 2♣ – 2◇ – 2NT is the only way to stop short of game after a Two Club opening.

(C) ♠ AQJ65
 ♡ A
 ◇ AKQ3
 ♣ AJ3

(D) ♠ AKQ432
 ♡ AKJ3
 ◇ A4
 ♣ 3

Both these hands are full-value Two Club openers. Hand (C) has 25 HCP and although game is by no means certain, if partner has as little as three small cards in spades game will have fair play, at worst depending on a 3-2 spade break and a 3-3 diamond break. Although Hand (D) has only 21 HCP, it has great playing strength, and again three small spades and nothing else would give game fair play.

(E) ♠ AK43
 ♡ AQJ5
 ◇ AK4
 ♣ AJ

(F) ♠ AKQJ1043
 ♡ AK32
 ◇ A
 ♣ 4

Hand (E) is too strong to let partner out below game. Open Two Clubs and rebid Three No-Trumps.

Hand (F) is so strong that you need little from partner to make a slam. Jump to Three Spades on the next round. This sets spades as trumps and asks him if he has an ace. If he has he bids it, otherwise he bids Three No-Trumps when he has a king or a singleton (outside spades), or Four Spades as a complete denial.

Lesson 131
Responding to Two Clubs

The old-fashioned requirements for making a *positive* response to an Acol Two Clubs were an ace and a king. Otherwise you were supposed to bid a Two Diamond negative, though a Two No-Trump response was allowed to show 8–10 points without an ace and a king. However, there are several problems with this style of response:

(1) If a response in a suit shows an ace and a king and Two No-Trumps denies, that is all very well if you have an unbalanced hand with an ace and a king or a balanced hand without. But what do you do if you have an unbalanced hand without an ace and a king or a balanced hand with an ace and a king?

(2) It is important not to push the auction to an uncomfortably high level before you know where you are going. Look at the following pair of hands:

```
  ♠ AK4    ┌─────┐   ♠ 652
  ♡ AQJ3   │  N  │   ♡ K1065
  ◇ 6      │W   E│   ◇ A9543
  ♣ AKQ54  │  S  │   ♣ 5
           └─────┘
```

Consider these two auctions:

(A) 2♣ 3◇   (B) 2♣ 2◇
    ?   3♣ 3◇
                    3♡ ?

On auction (A), opener really doesn't know whether to introduce his clubs at all. With a minimum Two Club opener and a singleton in his partner's suit it could well be right to bid Three No-Trumps. Maybe the heart fit would get lost altogether. On auction (B), however, opener has had the chance to bid both his suits and responder now knows he has a tremendous hand. He would be hard-pressed to find a Two Club opener where there would be no play for twelve tricks, so he can jump direct to the heart slam.

Our advice regarding giving a positive response to a Two Club opener is to be fairly freewheeling with Two Heart and Two Spade positives; you need about 7 or 8 points with a good suit. On the other hand, be very reticent about responding Two No-Trumps or Three of a minor. To respond Three of a minor you should have a good suit as well as an ace and a king.

A jump response in a suit over a Two Club opening shows a solid suit, not something either of us have been dealt in the whole of our playing careers, so don't expect it to crop up too often.

Lesson 132
Putting it into practice

Both vulnerable. Dealer North.

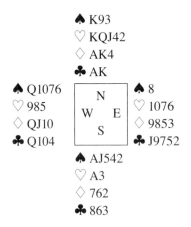

```
              ♠ K93
              ♡ KQJ42
              ◇ AK4
              ♣ AK
♠ Q1076                    ♠ 8
♡ 985        N            ♡ 1076
◇ QJ10    W     E         ◇ 9853
♣ Q104       S           ♣ J9752
              ♠ AJ542
              ♡ A3
              ◇ 762
              ♣ 863
```

South	West	North	East
–	–	2♣	Pass
2♠	Pass	2NT	Pass
3NT	Pass	6♠	All Pass

Contract: Six Spades by South
Lead: queen of diamonds

Even though South had two aces, his positive response made life difficult for his partner. Should North bid his hearts, support spades straightaway or show his balanced hand? In the event, he chose to show his balanced hand and South simply raised to game, showing a minimum positive response. North now knew that his side had more or less enough values for slam and could see that it would be a good contract facing AQxxx of spades and nothing else, so he simply bid Six Spades. Maybe someone should have bid Six No-Trumps but there was not a lot to choose between the two contracts.

Declarer won the diamond lead in the dummy, cashed the king of spades and played towards his ace-jack. When East showed out declarer was one down. Can you see how declarer could have done better?

His handling of the trump suit was very poor. There is a 100% line of play to bring in that spade suit for one loser provided it is not 5-0.

You need to forget all that you have learned about finesses. Win the ace of diamonds, play a spade to your ace and then a spade towards dummy's king-nine. If West follows low you put in the nine. If this loses to the ten or the queen, cashing the king next time will draw the remaining trump; if the nine holds with East showing out, cashing the king will leave West with just one trump winner. If, on the other hand, West shows out on the second round of spades, you rise with dummy's king and play dummy's last spade towards your jack. Deal the hand out for yourself and see how it works.

Lesson 133
The jump shift response

In Part II we looked at the initial response to One of a suit. We considered simple responses in a new suit, and simple and jump responses in no-trumps. What we neglected to cover then was a *jump bid* in a new suit.

A jump bid in a new suit shows a strong hand, say about 16 HCP or the equivalent in playing strength. It wakes partner up to the likelihood of there being a slam. However, just as we have said before, it is not generally a good idea to consume a lot of bidding space unless you know where you are going. To make a jump shift you need one of three hand-types:

(1) a strong single-suited hand
(2) a strong hand with a fit for partner
(3) a strong balanced hand

If you have type (1) you intend to rebid your suit, if you have type (2) you intend to support partner on the next round, and if you hand type (3) you intend to rebid in no-trumps.

The following would be suitable hands for a jump shift of Two Spades after partner has opened One Diamond:

(A)♠ KQJ1065 (B)♠ AQJ54
   ♡ A4   ♡ A3
   ♢ Q4   ♢ AK65
   ♣ AQ4   ♣ 54

At your next turn, with Hand (A) you would rebid Three Spades and with Hand (B) you would raise diamonds.

(C)♠ KQ1065 (D)♠ AK762
   ♡ AQ3   ♡ 3
   ♢ 54   ♢ AQ652
   ♣ AK2   ♣ 65

With Hand (C) you would rebid Three No-Trumps. Hand (D) is a borderline force, but the excellent diamond fit means that the hand has a great deal of playing strength. It is not hard to think of some very minimum hands for partner where slam is extremely good. Another reason for starting with a jump shift is that the hand will not be easy to bid otherwise. Say you respond One Spade and partner rebids Two Clubs or Two Diamonds. There is no easy way for you to show your diamond support and make a forcing bid. Our recommendation is to make an initial jump shift of Two Spades on this hand-type and support partner's diamonds on the next round.

Lesson 134
More on jump shifts

In the last lesson we looked at several hands that were suitable for making an initial jump shift, after partner has opened One Diamond. Here are some that are not:

(A) ♠ KQJ76   (B) ♠ AKJ104
    ♡ A2   ♡ 653
    ◇ 5   ◇ A3
    ♣ AKQ54   ♣ AQ2

Neither of these hands are suitable for a jump shift. On Hand (A) you are very poorly placed after the sequence 1◇ – 2♠ – 3◇. You would have to go to the four level to show your club suit (and as we will see later, a Four Club bid by you at this stage would not be natural). You should not make a jump shift with a two-suiter. Start with One Spade.

The problem with Hand (B) is if partner rebids Three Diamonds. It is not really satisfactory to rebid Three No-Trumps with no stopper in hearts and if you bid anything else partner will think you have an unbalanced hand. No, it is better to start with One Spade and see what happens.

So, what does opener rebid after his partner makes a jump shift?

In general, he should make the same rebid he would have made without the jump-shift but a level higher. So he rebids no-trumps with a balanced hand that was too strong to open One No-Trump. Otherwise he rebids his own suit or a new suit if it is lower-ranking than the one opened. It is generally not a good idea to make a higher bid than a simple rebid in the suit opened because you might make it difficult for responder to tell you why he has made a jump shift.

Suppose you open One Diamond on one of the following hands, and partner responds Two Hearts. What would you rebid?

(C) ♠ AQ43   (D) ♠ AQ3
    ♡ 4   ♡ Q54
    ◇ KQJ76   ◇ AQJ5
    ♣ J54   ♣ Q63

With Hand (C) rebid Two Spades. You know partner does not have four spades (he would not make a jump shift with a two-suiter), but it describes your hand well and may help him to evaluate his hand. He will now probably rebid Three Hearts (which you would raise to Four Hearts), Two No-Trumps (which you would raise to Three No-Trumps) or Three Diamonds which would make slam prospects a little stronger (the simple approach would be to show a little encouragement by raising to Four Diamonds – don't forget the auction cannot stop below game).

With Hand (D), simply rebid Two No-Trumps showing a balanced 15–17. It is unlikely that you will stop below slam now but you should conserve as much space as possible by keeping the bidding low. You can show your heart support on the next round.

Lesson 135
Putting it into practice

Now it is time to look at the bidding and play of a whole deal:

North-South vulnerable. Dealer South.

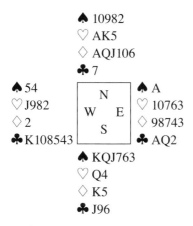

```
              ♠ 10982
              ♡ AK5
              ◇ AQJ106
              ♣ 7
  ♠ 54           N      ♠ A
  ♡ J982     W      E   ♡ 10763
  ◇ 2            S      ◇ 98743
  ♣ K108543             ♣ AQ2
              ♠ KQJ763
              ♡ Q4
              ◇ K5
              ♣ J96
```

South	West	North	East
1♠	Pass	3◇	Pass
3♠	Pass	5♠	All Pass

Contract: Five Spades by South
Lead: two of diamonds

We are going to look at special techniques for bidding slams in the next few lessons and we do not want to jump the gun. By the end of this course of lessons we are sure you would bid this hand differently. Here North felt he had too much simply to sign off in Four Spades and all he could think of to do was jump to Five Spades to ask his partner

if he had anything extra. Although South had a good spade suit, he was minimum and the rest of his hand was unexciting so he decided to call a halt.

Declarer won the king of diamonds lead and played the king of spades. East won with the ace and gave his partner a diamond ruff. West switched to a club and Five Spades was one down. North came in for some sharp criticism for his enthusiastic bidding.

Do you see where declarer went wrong?

The two of diamonds lead should have made South very suspicious. It is not normal to lead dummy's suit on this type of auction. After all, there are two unbid suits which would usually offer better prospects. If the two of diamonds is a singleton, declarer needs to discard his remaining card in the suit prior to drawing trumps.

This is how the play should have gone. Win the king of diamond, play three rounds of hearts discarding a diamond from hand and only now play a spade. East wins his ace but when he plays a diamond, declarer ruffs high, draws trumps and claims the remainder (twelve tricks in total if the defenders have failed to cash their club).

This play of discarding a diamond in order to prevent the opponents taking a ruff is called a Scissors Coup and occurs quite frequently.

Lesson 136
Slam bidding

Two things are needed for a successful slam (let us assume we are talking about a small slam but similar principles apply when contracting for all thirteen tricks): (1) twelve tricks, and (2) no more than one loser.

Of course, (1) is more important than (2). If you have twelve tricks you may get away with it even when you have two top losers because the defenders may make the wrong lead. However, if you don't have twelve tricks you will never succeed whatever the lead.

Generally speaking, an opinion as to the likelihood of twelve tricks is formed early in the auction. Then later some special techniques can be employed to discover if there are two losers. Let's look at some hands:

(A) ♠ AQ3   ♠ KJ2
     ♡ KJ64   ♡ AQ2
     ◇ K982   ◇ A3
     ♣ 65   ♣ KQJ107

West	East
1NT	6NT

West has 12–14 HCP in a balanced hand; East has 20 with a good five-card suit. When you have balanced hands you generally need in the region of 33–34 HCP to make a small slam and 37–38 for a grand. (This is easy to remember: to make a small slam you cannot afford to be missing two aces – impossible with 33+ HCP – and for a grand slam you can't afford to be missing one ace – impossible with 37 HCP.) Here East knows the partnership has 32–34 and should go direct to the slam because of his good suit.

(B) ♠ A98542   ♠ Q763
     ♡ AK32   ♡ Q64
     ◇ 7   ◇ A652
     ♣ A4   ♣ K5

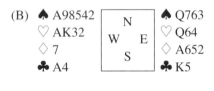

West	East
1♠	3♠
5♠	6♠

West's hand is very powerful once his partner has made a jump raise showing four-card support and 10–11 HCP. Until the next lesson there is nothing he can do to show his enthusiasm other than bid Five Spades, asking his partner to press on if he is maximum. East also likes his hand. He has an ace and a king as well as being at the top end of his range, so he presses on to the slam, which turns out to be an excellent contract.

Experts can debate for hours about the odds required for being in a slam at various vulnerabilities and forms of scoring but generally you should not bid a slam if it is less than an even-money shot. So if all it depends on is a finesse, it is borderline. If it needs more as well (perhaps some reasonable breaks) then you should not bid it.

Lesson 137
Blackwood

A useful aid to slam bidding was invented by an American, Easley Blackwood, who realised that it would be often be useful to know how many aces partner had. What he came up with was the following scheme.

When the partnership has an agreed trump suit, a bid of Four No-Trumps is conventional, asking partner how many aces he has. He responds as follows:

5♣	none (or four) aces
5♢	one ace
5♡	two aces
5♠	three aces

Once the Four No-Trump bidder has heard the reply, if all the aces are present he can continue with Five No-Trumps to ask for kings which are shown in a similar manner.

It should be noted that proceeding with Five No-Trumps *guarantees* that all the aces are present (why ask for kings when you are forced to a small slam and know you have insufficient ammunition for a grand?). Over Five No-Trumps, if partner has a good source of tricks he may simply bid the grand slam rather than show his kings.

Here are some examples:

(A) ♠ QJ762　　　　♠ AK1043
　　 ♡ A6　 N　　　♡ KQJ1054
　　 ♢ A532　W　E　♢ 6
　　 ♣ J2　 S　　　♣ 3

West	East
1♠	4NT
5♡	6♠

This is easy for Blackwood. When West opens One Spade, all East needs to know is how many aces West holds. When he shows up with two, East bids the excellent slam.

(B) ♠ AK6543　　　♠ Q7
　　 ♡ K8652　 N　♡ QJ1093
　　 ♢ A　W　E　　♢ KQJ3
　　 ♣ 6　 S　　　♣ K10

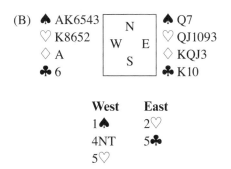

West	East
1♠	2♡
4NT	5♣
5♡	

One of Blackwood's strengths is that it can keep you out of no-play slams. Here East has 14 HCP for his Two Heart response but most of them are completely useless to West. West knows there are two aces missing so signs off in Five Hearts.

Hand (B) is a good example of the point we made in the previous lesson. Although there are two top losers and the slam should not be bid, at least there are twelve tricks and the slam would usually be made on a spade or diamond lead – declarer gets rid of his losing club on one of East's diamonds before tackling trumps.

Lesson 138
Cue-bidding

While Blackwood solves some of the problems of slam bidding, sometimes knowing how many aces your partner has is not the answer. Let's look at some hands:

(A)   ♠ AK7632   ♠ Q984
       ♡ KQ4   ♡ J103
       ◇ KQJ3   ◇ 65
       ♣ none   ♣ AK103

West	East
2♠	3♠
4♣	4♠
Pass	

Here there was no point whatsoever in West asking East how many aces he has. Only if he had none would the answer help at all.

Instead West *cue-bids* Four Clubs. When a trump suit is agreed, a bid in a new suit at the four level is not natural; rather, it shows a control (ace, king, void or singleton) and some slam interest. It suggests that partner should cue-bid in return if he also has slam interest.

East would cue-bid a red-suit ace if he had one, so West knows there is no slam.

(B)   ♠ A8542   ♠ K6
       ♡ K96   ♡ AQJ1065
       ◇ AJ43   ◇ 65
       ♣ 5   ♣ A62

West	East
1♠	2♡
3♡	4♣*
4◇*	4♠*
5♣*	6♡

* cue-bids

Here East's problem was the two losing diamonds. If he had asked West how many aces he had, what would he have done if the answer was 'one'? West might have had two top diamond losers as well. Again, the answer was to cue-bid.

East showed his ace of clubs and West his ace of diamonds. East was too good to sign off now. He could, if he had preferred, have used Blackwood now, having discovered the diamond control. That would have been a perfectly acceptable alternative auction. However, instead he proceeded with a Four Spade cue-bid and West showed his second-round club control. East had now heard enough and went straight to the small slam.

Different partnerships have different rules about whether you should cue-bid aces before kings or whether you just cue-bid 'up the line', not minding whether first or second-round control is held. Our advice to inexperienced players is to make sure your first cue-bid is a first-round control but thereafter to cue-bid second-round controls happily.

Lesson 139
More on slam bidding

There are two further conventional bids you may come across in slam bidding.

Gerber

Gerber is similar to Blackwood but the asking bid is Four Clubs not Four No-Trumps. Generally speaking, we would not recommend Gerber as it does not fit in very well with cue-bidding, which we believe to be a more valuable tool. However, there is one situation where Gerber works very well and that is directly over a no-trump opening bid.

Suppose partner opens One No-Trump and you hold:

(A)	♠ KJ5	(B)	♠ KQJ8743
	♡ AQ2		♡ A
	◇ K104		◇ KQJ5
	♣ AK105		♣ 6

With Hand (A), raise to Four No-Trumps, which is *quantitative*, asking partner to bid a slam if he is maximum. If Four No-Trumps is quantitative, what do you bid with Hand (B) when all you want to know is how many aces partner holds? The answer to that is Four Clubs, Gerber. If partner has no aces and bids Four Diamonds, or one ace and bids Four Hearts, you can sign off safely in Four Spades. If he has two aces he bids Four Spades and you bid the small slam. If he has three aces and responds Four No-Trumps you bid the grand slam.

If you sit down to play bridge with someone who has not read this book, be quite sure to make it clear that you play Gerber only directly over a One No-Trump or Two No-Trump opening.

Five No-Trumps

Sometimes after several cue-bids you know that your side has all the aces and kings necessary for a slam but you are unsure of the combined trump quality. In this situation Five No-Trumps is used to ask partner to bid a grand slam if he has two of the top three trump honours. Look at this pair of hands:

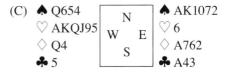

(C)	♠ Q654		N		♠ AK1072
	♡ AKQJ95	W		E	♡ 6
	◇ Q4		S		◇ A762
	♣ 5				♣ A43

West	East
1♡	1♠
3♠	4♣
4♡	5◇
5NT	7♠

After three cue-bids West knows that if his partner has the ace and king of spades as well as the minor-suit controls, a grand slam will be a good contract. So he bids Five No-Trumps, asking for two of the top honours. East is happy to oblige.

Lesson 140
Slams to bid and play 1

It will be much easier for you to see how slam bidding works properly when you get some real hands to bid and play. Don't forget to deal out the cards.

Both vulnerable. Dealer North.

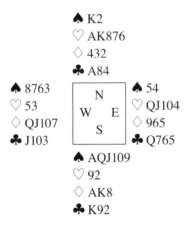

```
              ♠ K2
              ♡ AK876
              ◇ 432
              ♣ A84
  ♠ 8763    ┌─────────┐   ♠ 54
  ♡ 53      │    N    │   ♡ QJ104
  ◇ QJ107   │  W   E  │   ◇ 965
  ♣ J103    │    S    │   ♣ Q765
            └─────────┘
              ♠ AQJ109
              ♡ 92
              ◇ AK8
              ♣ K92
```

South	West	North	East
–	–	1♡	Pass
2♠	Pass	3♡	Pass
3NT	Pass	4NT	Pass
6♠	All Pass		

Contract: Six Spades by South
Lead: queen of diamonds

After South's jump shift, North rebid his hearts, as he would have done over a One Spade response. South bid Three No-Trumps to show his balanced hand-type.

North, with 14 HCP and good controls was too good to accept the sign-off. He raised to Four No-Trumps. This was not Blackwood (no suit had been agreed), but rather a simple quantitative raise, showing a balanced hand with extra values. South decided to accept the slam try and jumped to Six Spades because of his good suit quality.

Let us first suppose that the auction had ended up in the more ambitious Seven Spades. West leads the queen of diamonds.

Declarer should win in hand, draw trumps and then play the ace and king of hearts and ruff a heart. If that suit breaks 3-3 then he can cross back to dummy and discard his club and diamond losers on the established hearts.

In Seven Spades declarer needs to find the hearts 3-3; he needs *two* extra tricks in the suit to make a total of thirteen. However, the actual auction ended in Six Spades. Declarer should try to make twelve tricks rather than go for thirteen.

The correct line of play in Six Spades on a diamond lead is to win in hand, draw trumps and *duck* a heart. Win the diamond return and now cash the ace and king of hearts and ruff a heart. This establishes the suit even if they are 4-2, and declarer can cross back to dummy with the ace of clubs to enjoy the long heart.

Lesson 141
Slams to bid and play 2

No-one vulnerable. Dealer South.

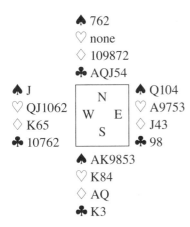

```
                ♠ 762
                ♡ none
                ◇ 109872
                ♣ AQJ54
   ♠ J          ┌─────┐      ♠ Q104
   ♡ QJ1062     │  N  │      ♡ A9753
   ◇ K65        │W   E│      ◇ J43
   ♣ 10762      │  S  │      ♣ 98
                └─────┘
                ♠ AK9853
                ♡ K84
                ◇ AQ
                ♣ K3
```

South	West	North	East
2♠	Pass	3♣	Pass
3NT	Pass	4♠	Pass
4NT	Pass	5◇	Pass
6♠	All Pass		

Contract: Six Spades by South
Lead: queen of hearts

Again, let's look at the auction a bid at a time. South is just about worth an Acol Two Spades, though it is stretching a little. North's decision to make a positive bid of Three Clubs was a good one. Although he is minimum in terms of high cards for such a bid, his three-card spade support and void heart are likely to be extremely useful. South rebid Three No-Trumps to show a fairly balanced hand with stoppers in the other suits, but it was clear for North to remove to Four Spades with his three-card support. This made South's hand very much better. He could see the probability of his partner's black-suit holdings being as they were, so he bid Four No-Trumps.

There are various schemes around concerning how to respond to Blackwood when you have a void but our experience is that unless partner can know where the void is there is not much point showing him that you have one (unless the partnership has all four aces, he will not be sure that your void is not facing one of his aces). Here North is best simply to obey orders and show his one ace. This is enough for South to bid the slam.

In the play South ruffed the heart lead in the dummy, cashed the ace and king of spades and started on the clubs. However, East ruffed the third round and declarer eventually went two down.

The correct play is simple when you see it. Ruff the opening lead and duck a trump. The advantage of this play is that declarer loses a trump trick while dummy still has a trump to protect declarer's heart weakness. Win the return, draw trumps and cash the club suit. Once again, it is important to focus on the contract you are in. Had North-South bid the grand slam, a 2-2 trump break would have been necessary and declarer's actual line of play would have been correct.

Lesson 142
Slams to bid and play 3

On this hand you must always lose one trick but need to make sure you don't lose two.

East-West vulnerable. Dealer South.

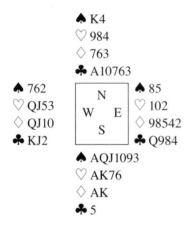

```
                    ♠ K4
                    ♡ 984
                    ◇ 763
                    ♣ A10763
    ♠ 762                       ♠ 85
    ♡ QJ53        N             ♡ 102
    ◇ QJ10     W     E          ◇ 98542
    ♣ KJ2         S             ♣ Q984
                    ♠ AQJ1093
                    ♡ AK76
                    ◇ AK
                    ♣ 5
```

South	West	North	East
2♣	Pass	2◇	Pass
2♠	Pass	3♣	Pass
3♡	Pass	3♠	Pass
4♠	Pass	5♣	Pass
6♠	All Pass		

Contract: Six Spades by South
Lead: queen of diamonds

Although North has an ace and king, a Three Club response takes up a great deal of space and may make it difficult for South to describe his hand, so we recommend starting with Two Diamonds. South shows his spades and North his clubs. When South introduces his hearts, North gives preference to spades and South, with a minimum Two Club opener, simply raises to game. Since the Three Spade preference would usually be made with a doubleton in support, the Four Spade raise would generally show a six-card suit, otherwise South would be more likely to rebid in no-trumps. With an ace and a king when he has promised nothing at all, North must make a forward-going move, so cue-bids his ace of clubs. This is enough for South who expects North to have something useful in one of the majors to justify his enthusiasm.

In the play declarer could see that the slam would be no problem if hearts broke 3-3. So, he won the lead and rattled off all his trumps but one, hoping that if hearts were 4-2 then someone might discard one. Of course, this was a vain hope when he had actually bid the suit. West held on to all his hearts and the slam eventually went one down.

It was perhaps not obvious that dummy, with its doubleton spade and trebleton heart, had a ruffing value. However, all that declarer needed to do was win the diamond lead and play out ace, king and another heart. He could then win the return, ruff a heart with dummy's king of spades and claim the remainder.

Note that declarer was lucky West did not lead a trump, which would have doomed the slam when hearts did not break.

Part VII
A Few More Things You Need To Know

This section is a miscellany of bits and pieces that do not really fit in anywhere else.

Lesson 143
Pre-emptive openings

We have now covered all opening bids up to the level of Two No-Trumps. What about the rest? Theoretically there are 35 possible opening bids (five denominations times seven levels) and we have dealt with only ten. In practice, the ten we have dealt with cover more than 90% of opening bids. As opening bids get higher and higher the frequency of occurrence gets lower and lower. Neither of us has ever made an opening bid at the seven level, and only one or two at the six level.

Three- and four-level openings, however, crop up with reasonable frequency. These bids show hands with long strong suits, with good playing strength but little defence. They are referred to as *pre-emptive* bids. The idea is that the high level of the opening makes it difficult for the opponents to do the right thing. Because of the danger of going for a penalty, the playing strength required depends on the prevailing vulnerability.

Here are some examples:

(A)♠ KQJ10762   (B)♠ 65
   ♡ 652   ♡ 82
   ◇ 43   ◇ AKJ10762
   ♣ 7   ♣ 43

On Hand (A) open Three Spades unless you are vulnerable against not. With Hand (B) open Three Diamonds at any vulnerability.

The general rule is that if the worst comes to the worst you should not go for more than an 800 penalty if the opponents are vulnerable and not more than 500 if they are non-vulnerable. These figures roughly equate to the value of the opponents' vulnerable game. Remember that the worst hand your partner can have for you is not a complete bust; the worst is when he has nothing to help you make any tricks but enough to prevent the opponents making their contract.

Here are examples of four-level openings:

(C)♠ 65   (D)♠ KQJ10652
   ♡ 3   ♡ 65
   ◇ 82   ◇ KJ102
   ♣ KJ1096532 ♣ –

A four-level opening bid in a minor typically shows a non-solid eight-card suit. If the suit was solid there would be some danger in bypassing Three No-Trumps. Here, with Hand (C) open Three Clubs vulnerable, but Four Clubs non-vulnerable. The higher the level at which you make your opponents guess, the more often they will go wrong. With Hand (D) open Four Spades at any vulnerability. It would be more or less impossible to conduct a scientific auction with this type of hand. How can you tell partner that the queen of diamonds is the most important card in the pack for you? You might easily find that you can make Four Spades when the opponents can make their game (or even slam) as well.

Lesson 144
More on pre-emptive openings

Because pre-emptive openings describe such a specific hand-type and because the level of the auction is already high, there is not a great deal to be said about responding to them. If you are not going to pass, it is usually right either to raise partner or bid Three No-Trumps, but you may be surprised which type of hand is suitable for which action. Suppose your partner opens Three Hearts, vulnerable, and you hold:

(A) ♠ A65
    ♡ K53
    ♢ A1087
    ♣ QJ4

(B) ♠ KQJ76
    ♡ 7
    ♢ A1092
    ♣ AJ2

What would you bid?

With Hand (A) you bid Three No-Trumps and with Hand (B) you raise him to Four Hearts. You expect him to hold something like AQJ10xxx in hearts and little else. If you hold Hand (A) you expect to win the opening lead and run off nine tricks. There could easily be four losers in Four Hearts.

On Hand (B) if the heart suit does not come in you could be in severe trouble in Three No-Trumps as partner is unlikely to have an entry. However, in Four Hearts, when you have knocked out the ace of spades you should be able to make, in total, six hearts, two spades and two aces.

There is one further pre-emptive opening bid you might come across:

A Three No-Trump opening bid

This opening cannot show a balanced hand because if you were too strong to open Two No-Trumps you would open Two Clubs. A Three No-Trump opening is generally played to show a long solid minor with little outside (unless facing a passed partner when you can hold more or less whatever you like as partner is not expected to bid over it). If partner has enough high cards to suggest that Three No-Trumps might make he passes, otherwise he should remove to Four Clubs, which opener passes if that is his suit or converts to Four Diamonds. Suppose partner opens Three No-Trumps and you hold:

(C) ♠ J105
    ♡ A10965
    ♢ 6
    ♣ A762

(D) ♠ 54
    ♡ KQ52
    ♢ QJ105
    ♣ 652

With Hand (C) pass Three No-Trumps which is a fair gamble though you are taking a chance with the spade suit. With Hand (D) remove to Four Clubs. You would expect to lose at least seven tricks in Three No-Trumps whereas Four Clubs may well go only one down.

Of course, you should *always* remove Three No-Trumps when you have a void in a minor. You know that in no-trumps you will not be able to reach his hand.

Lesson 145
Defending against pre-empts 1

If you play in bridge circles that include players who have not read this book you may come across several different defences to pre-emptive openings. However, against three-level openings the defensive method that we will recommend here, and the one that is in most common use at tournament level worldwide, is a straightforward take-out double. Just as over a one-level opening bid, a double asks partner to bid his best suit.

Against higher level openings, a double shows any hand with above opening-bid values and with no extreme distribution. The partner of the doubler should tend to leave the double in unless he has good distribution of his own.

Here are a couple of examples of doubles of a Three Spade opener:

(A) ♠ 76　　　(B) ♠ none
　　 ♡ AK76　　　 ♡ KQ105
　　 ◇ A1065　　　 ◇ AQJ98
　　 ♣ KJ3　　　 ♣ KJ76

Both these hands should double a Three Spade opener.

You may be feeling extremely nervous about doubling, particularly on Hand (A). Perhaps you are thinking that partner might hold nothing and you might be about to go for a large penalty. It is true that that is a risk, but that is why your right-hand opponent has opened Three Spades, to make

you guess. On Hand (A) you hold 15 HCP. Let us assume that the Three Spade opener holds 7 HCP. That leaves 18 HCP for your partner and left-hand opponent. So, on average your partner will hold 9 HCP, giving your side 24 and some prospects of making game if you have a fit. One thing is certain: if you pass, he will not bid when he has 9 or 10 HCP.

There are two further points to remember when bidding over a pre-empt:

(1) You should assume your partner has 7 or 8 HCP. If you would want to be in the action if that is what he has, then you bid. Conversely, if you hold 7 or 8 HCP and partner bids over a pre-empt, you should not get too excited. Remember that he has already assumed you hold that much.

(2) If bidding Three No-Trumps is one of your options, go for it. When one hand has a seven-card suit, then it is quite likely that there are bad breaks about which may scupper any suit contract you bid. Also, suppose you hold Axx in the suit opened; because the pre-emptor tends to have little outside his long suit, once you have ducked a round or two of this suit, you can cut that player out of the game completely and make your contract by losing tricks to his partner's hand.

Lesson 146
Defending against pre-empts 2

In the last lesson we talked a lot about the principles involved in defending against pre-empts. Let's look at a couple of hands you might hold when your partner doubles a Three Diamond opening:

(A) ♠ J873
   ♡ AQ5
   ◇ A106
   ♣ Q65

(B) ♠ KJ1065
   ♡ 873
   ◇ K6
   ♣ J87

With Hand (A) bid Three No-Trumps. Yes, of course, partner might hold four spades, but even if he does the suit might break badly. You have sufficient values to expect to make game. If the pre-emptor leads his long suit you can duck a couple of rounds and then with any luck he will not be able to get in before you have established nine tricks.

With Hand (B) settle for Three Spades. The ace of diamonds is probably over your king so your left-hand opponents will probably lead something else, through your partner's holding. Remember, partner is already hoping you have 7 or 8 HCP when he doubles. If partner passes Three Spades you are unlikely to have missed anything.

Of course, if you want to bid over the pre-empt there are other bids available than double. You can bid a decent suit of your own, or else bid Three No-Trumps yourself. Again, assume a Three Diamond opening.

(C) ♠ AQJ1065
   ♡ A76
   ◇ 6
   ♣ J106

(D) ♠ K5
   ♡ KQ65
   ◇ A106
   ♣ AJ106

With Hand (C) bid Three Spades. This shows more or less opening-bid values and a decent five-card or longer suit. Again you have assumed partner holds 7 or 8 useful HCP, so he should not bid on unless he has more than that.

Hand (D) is of the type where many players often err. It is wrong to make a take-out double on this hand. You have a balanced 17-count. Bid Three No-Trumps. While it is true that partner may have a heart fit and Four Hearts may play better than Three No-Trumps, it is much more likely that partner has spade length and responds Three Spades or Four Spades. Even if Four Hearts is a better game, you may be able to make Three No-Trumps by ducking a couple of rounds of diamonds. Yes, of course it is dangerous to bid Three No-Trumps all on your own with only 17 HCP, but that is why people pre-empt. If your partner has his fair share of values you should have 25 between you, and the pre-empt should help you plan the play.

Lesson 147
Putting it into practice

No-one vulnerable. Dealer East.

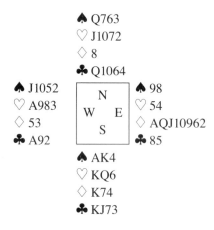

```
              ♠ Q763
              ♡ J1072
              ◇ 8
              ♣ Q1064
♠ J1052      ┌──────┐   ♠ 98
♡ A983       │  N   │   ♡ 54
◇ 53         │ W  E │   ◇ AQJ10962
♣ A92        │  S   │   ♣ 85
             └──────┘
              ♠ AK4
              ♡ KQ6
              ◇ K74
              ♣ KJ73
```

South	West	North	East
–	–	–	3◇
3NT	All Pass		

Contract: Three No-Trumps by South
Lead: five of diamonds to East's ten

South did not mess around after the Three Diamond opening. He quite correctly bid Three No-Trumps on his balanced hand. If he had doubled, North would have bid Three of one of the majors and South still would not have known whether to pass, raise or bid Three No-Trumps.

In the play declarer did not shine, however. He won the diamond lead with the king and played a club. West won his ace straight away and played a second diamond.

East cashed his six winners in the suit and then played a heart so West made his ace there as well. Declarer went four down.

East had done well not to play his ace of diamonds at trick one. He did not know that his partner had another diamond but it was his best chance. Dummy's holdings in the other suits suggested that there was nowhere else for the defence to go for tricks.

Declarer, however, should have done better. If he had held Axx in diamonds he would have ducked a couple of rounds as a matter of routine. It should have been just as routine to duck holding the king, though of course he could afford to duck only one round. If declarer ducks the first round of diamonds the defence can do no better than cash the ace and play another diamond. Declarer wins and knocks out the ace of clubs. When West wins, there is nothing he can do. Whatever he plays, there is time for declarer to knock out the ace of hearts and make in total three spades, two hearts, one diamond and three clubs. That play at trick one made four tricks difference.

Lesson 148
Stayman 1

A *conventional* bid is a bid whose meaning is not natural. For example, a take-out double is *conventional*, as is the strong, artificial way in which we use a Two Club opening – it has nothing to do with clubs.

We are not going to burden you with many conventions, but one that is played by most players all over the world is Stayman. This is a device to locate a 4-4 major-suit fit after a One No-Trump or Two No-Trump opening.

Over the One No-Trump opening responder bids Two Clubs (or Three Clubs over Two No-Trumps), which is forcing and asks opener if he has a four-card major. The responses are:

2◇ 'No, I don't have a four-card major'
2♡ 'I have four hearts (and may have four spades as well)'
2♠ 'I have four spades but don't have four hearts.

We will look at some pairs of hands to see Stayman at work:

(A)

	♠ AK54		♠ Q1076
	♡ 65	N	♡ A7
	◇ KJ42	W E	◇ Q103
	♣ Q103	S	♣ KJ92

West	East
1NT	2♣
2♠	4♠

Over the One No-Trump, East bids Two Clubs to see if there is a 4-4 spade fit. When West shows his four-card suit, East raises to Four Spades. As you can see this is a good contract which will make provided spades break 3-2 and no-one can get a ruff in a minor suit. Three No-Trumps, which is where you would have played before you had heard of Stayman, is hopeless. The defenders are bound to lead a heart and will eventually take at least four hearts and two minor-suit aces to beat Three No-Trumps by two tricks or more.

(B)

	♠ 65		♠ KQJ3
	♡ Q105	N	♡ KJ93
	◇ KQJ6	W E	◇ 107
	♣ AQ93	S	♣ J102

West	East
1NT	2♣
2◇	2NT
3NT	

With both four-card majors, East tries Two Clubs. West makes the denial bid of Two Diamonds. Now East bids Two No-Trumps, which is a non-forcing limit bid, just as if he had raised to Two No-Trumps directly. With a maximum, West presses on to the game. On this hand you have ended up exactly where you would have done without Stayman.

Lesson 149
Stayman 2

You do not need a strong hand to use Stayman but you do need to know what you are going to bid next. The following weak hands are suitable for Stayman:

(A) ♠ 9843　　(B) ♠ J10976
　　♡ 8732　　　　♡ J1065
　　◇ 9843　　　　◇ 54
　　♣ 7　　　　　♣ 72

On Hand (A) you bid Two Clubs and pass whatever partner says. There is a slight risk that his distribution is 3-3-2-5 with five clubs and only two diamonds, but that is a risk worth taking. You know that One No-Trump is going to be dreadful and you are probably about to be doubled. Using Stayman gives you a good chance of avoiding trouble.

With Hand (B) bid Two Clubs. If partner bids Two of a major you pass happily. If he bids Two Diamonds bid Two Spades. This is a weakness take-out, just like an immediate Two Spade bid, but this time you were able to investigate a heart fit as well.

(C) ♠ 76　　　　(D) ♠ Q1032
　　♡ 872　　　　　♡ J103
　　◇ 63　　　　　◇ 3
　　♣ QJ10965　　♣ QJ1096

When you use a bid as a convention, you can't use in its natural sense. When you have a hand on which you would have liked to make a weakness take-out into clubs you have to bid Two Clubs and then Three Clubs. Partner should always pass.

Hand (D) is not so clear, but there is quite a case for bidding Two Clubs. If partner bids Two of a major you can pass. Two Hearts may be a 4-3 fit but that may still play better than One No-Trump. If partner bids Two Diamonds, you bid Three Clubs and partner will pass. This may be a 5-2 fit, it is true, but you have given yourself a good chance of improving the contract.

(E) ♠ Q843　　(F) ♠ Q843
　　♡ 7　　　　　♡ K732
　　◇ K843　　　◇ 7
　　♣ Q732　　　♣ Q843

Neither of these hands is suitable for Stayman. It is true that if partner responds Two Diamonds or Two Spades and you have Hand (E) you will be happy. But what if he bids Two Hearts? With Hand (F) you would be happy if he responded in a major but what if he bids Two Diamonds? It is best to pass One No-Trump and hope for the best.

Should you have been dealt a very weak hand, so you know the next hand is about to double, it could work well to bid Two Clubs on less than ideal distribution. Even if you do not find a fit, it may be harder for the opponents to double you because they may not realise you are weak.

Lesson 150
Putting it into practice

Here's a whole hand. Remember to deal it out.

Both vulnerable. Dealer South.

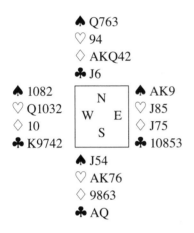

```
              ♠ Q763
              ♡ 94
              ◇ AKQ42
              ♣ J6
♠ 1082                      ♠ AK9
♡ Q1032      N             ♡ J85
◇ 10      W     E          ◇ J75
♣ K9742      S             ♣ 10853
              ♠ J54
              ♡ AK76
              ◇ 9863
              ♣ AQ
```

South	West	North	East
1NT	Pass	2♣	Pass
2♡	Pass	3NT	All Pass

Contract: Three No-Trumps by South
Lead: four of clubs

Over the One No-Trump opening North hoped there might be a 4-4 spade fit, so he bid Two Clubs, Stayman. When South bid Two Hearts he jumped to Three No-Trumps on the strength of his good five-card diamond suit.

Suppose that South had had four cards in spades as well as four hearts. What should he have done? Well, he would have known that his partner had four spades because otherwise he would not have used Stayman. So if he South had four spades as well he should have bid Four Spades over Three No-Trumps. *Bidding Two Clubs, Stayman, guarantees a four-card major* (except in the sequence 1NT – 2♣ – 2 any – 3♣).

In the play declarer won the club lead and was happy to see that he had nine tricks on top. He played a low diamond to dummy's ace, cashed the king and now the play slowed considerably. When the suit broke 3-1 he realised that he could not cash all his winners. If he cashed the queen, he would have the nine left in hand and just the four and two in the dummy. He did his best by cashing the queen of diamonds, playing a diamond to his nine and now a low heart towards the jack (he could see that playing on spades would not help him). However, West jumped in with the queen and cleared the clubs. Now declarer could get to dummy with the jack of hearts to cash his long diamond, but then could not get back to hand to make his ace and king of hearts. Whatever he did he was one down.

Declarer should have played a little more carefully at trick two. He should have led the *nine* of diamonds to dummy's ace, then played the *eight* under dummy's king, and then the *six* under dummy's queen. That would have left the four and two in dummy and the three in his hand. As long as he cashed the four first he would be in the right hand for the fifth diamond.

Lesson 151
Cue-bidding the opponents' suit

In Lesson 115 we said if you had length and strength in the suit overcalled by the opposition you should make a penalty double and that a bid of that suit would not be natural.

This bid in an opponent's suit is called a *cue-bid* and it can crop up in a number of different sequences. It usually shows a strong hand with no easy natural bid. Such a hand is usually (semi-) balanced without good stoppers in the opponent's suit.

Here are a few example sequences:

(A) ♠ 6 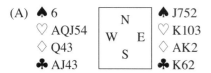 ♠ J752
♡ AQJ54 ♡ K103
◇ Q43 ◇ AK2
♣ AJ43 ♣ K62

South	West	North	East
–	1♡	1♠	2♠
Pass	3♣	Pass	3♡
Pass	4♡	All Pass	

After the One Spade overcall, East did not like to bid Three No-Trumps with so little in spades, so instead he cue-bid Two Spades. West showed his second suit and now East could show his three-card heart support which West raised to game.

(B) ♠ 652 ♠ K104
♡ AKJ5 ♡ 76
◇ Q3 ◇ AKJ54
♣ AQJ3 ♣ 872

South	West	North	East
–	1♡	1♠	2◇
Pass	2♠	Pass	2NT
Pass	3NT	All Pass	

East's Two diamond bid gave West a problem. He had enough for game after a two-level response, but he had only four hearts and no real diamond support. If he had bid Three Clubs it would have sounded as if he had an unbalanced hand. Instead, he cue-bid Two Spades. Now East bid his stopper and the good no-trump game was reached.

(C) ♠ AK542 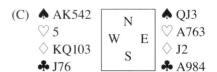 ♠ QJ3
♡ 5 ♡ A763
◇ KQ103 ◇ J2
♣ J76 ♣ A984

South	West	North	East
1♡	1♠	Pass	2♡
Pass	3◇	Pass	4♠
All Pass			

A jump raise of an overcall shows four trumps and not a terribly strong hand. So, what do you do when you have only three trumps but a hand too good to raise to Two? This is the only situation in which a cue-bid is not forcing to game. If partner is minimum he will simply rebid his suit. If, as here, he has a good hand he will bid a new suit and you can bid game.

Lesson 152
Don't make it too easy

Because bridge is a partnership game you should constantly be on the look-out for situations where you can make life easy for your partner or difficult for your opponents. When you are defending it is more important to help your partner than to mislead declarer. Back in Lesson 58 we looked at how to play as a defender with touching honours. You will probably play against defenders who think it is clever to win with the ace when they have the ace and king, or with the king when they have the king and queen. However, in our experience such plays serve to mislead partner much more often than declarer. If you play true cards as a defender you will defeat more contracts and be a more popular partner.

However, when you are declarer it is a completely different matter. Now there is no partner to deceive.

Look at the following situation where you are declarer in Three No-Trumps:

```
              764
2 led     [          ]     Q played
              AK
```

What will the defenders think if you play the ace? They will think that you also hold the king, because they will think that you would duck at least one round if you held only the ace. What about if you win with the king? East will not know whether you or his partner holds the ace. West will think you have the ace, but may consider the possibility that his partner has the ace and is defending in the way suggested in Lesson 73.

So, if this is your weakest suit and you would like your opponents to switch you should win with the ace, letting them know that you also have the king. On the other hand, if there is a wide-open suit that you don't want your opponents to switch to then you should win with the king.

Now consider the same suit lay-out, but this time it is a side suit in a suit contract.

```
              764
2 led     [          ]     Q played
              AK
```

Now if you win with the king, both defenders will know that you also hold the ace because West would not underlead an ace against a suit contract, and East would have played the ace if he had held it. If you win the ace, there may be doubt in both their minds as to who holds the king. So, if you want them to continue this suit when they next get the lead, win with the ace; if you want them to switch, win with the king.

Of course, these deceptive efforts will not work all the time, or not even most of the time, but they do give the opponents more opportunities to go wrong.

Lesson 153
More on making life difficult

In the last lesson we looked at whether declarer should win a trick with the ace or the king. Similar logic applies when he has the king and the queen:

```
                764
2 led        [          ]   J played
                KQ3
```

Against a no-trump contract, if you win with the queen, West will place you with the king because he knows his partner would play the king if he had it; East will guess that you have either the ace or the king because his partner may have chosen to lead a top card if he had both ace and king. If you win with the king, both opponents may think the other has the queen. Your correct play will depend on the whole hand and whether or not you would like this suit to be continued.

Of course, this situation would not arise in a suit contract for West would not underlead an ace and East would play the ace if he held it.

There are similar plays that can be made with small cards. Consider this lay-out:

```
                764
A led        [          ]   5 played
                Q1083
```

Suppose, first, that you were playing in a no-trump contract. It looks as if West has decided to lead a top heart from an original holding of AKJ92 or maybe AKJ2. This would not be a bad idea (on some other lay-out) if he also held an outside entry. You suspect East's five is a singleton and would like to encourage West to continue the suit. If you play the three, West will know that East has played his lowest card, i.e. has been discouraging. However, if you play the eight (or even the ten), West may think his partner has the three and has played the five from an original holding of Q53, in which case he may continue the suit.

Now imagine that you are playing in a suit contract and this is a side-suit. If you would like West to switch you play your lowest card, so West knows that East has played a low card. If you would like West to continue you play a high card, to make it look as if East has the low card(s) you have concealed.

This may all sound very confusing, but read through it again and try to follow the logic. For once, there is a very simple rule for you to follow to get this sort of play right: *as declarer you should play the same card that you would do if you were a defender.* So, if you, as declarer, like the lead, you 'encourage' (i.e. play a high card), but if you don't like the lead, you 'discourage' (i.e. play a low card). This will soon get you a reputation for being a difficult opponent.

Lesson 154
Ethics

All club and tournament bridge is governed to by the Laws of Contract Bridge. Many of these laws apply to subjects such as revokes, leads out of turn, insufficient bids etc. The laws of rubber bridge are covered in the book *The International Laws of Contract Bridge*. Duplicate bridge, which we have not covered in this book, has a similar set of rules: *The Laws of Duplicate Contract Bridge*. Both are availalble from the English Bridge Union, Broadfields, Bicester Road, Aylesbury HP19 8AZ; tel: 01296 317200. Most bridge clubs will have a copy of one of these books and also someone in charge to look up the relevant penalty for you. However, most people who play bridge at home generally ignore these laws. If someone plays from the wrong hand they are told to pick up their card and play from the right one. Similarly, it is normal to let someone off with a revoke unless it has actually cost the non-offending side a trick. If you make an insufficient bid, then you change it.

However, there is another type of offence entirely, that which falls under the general heading of *ethics*.

When you start to play bridge you are slower to bid or play when you have a problem than when you don't. Maybe you look disappointed if as a defender partner does not lead the suit you want, or you look enthusiastic when he does. When you are bidding perhaps you use different voice inflections when you are happy to make a bid than when you are not. Maybe you double loudly when you are sure a contract is going off and more hesitantly when you would like partner to feel free to remove it.

When you are learning, all this sort of behaviour is acceptable. Indeed, many people who play bridge in their own homes are guilty of this type of behaviour all the time and if everyone is happy with it, then that is fine.

But ... IT REALLY ISN'T DONE.

If you do this type of thing in unfamiliar company, or at a bridge club, it is quite likely that someone will get cross with you. They may even accuse you of cheating and a nasty row may well develop.

The way bridge should be played is in an even tempo with all bids being spoken in the same manner. Your partner should not be able to tell from your expression whether you are pleased or displeased with the suit he has led. In the bidding, if your partner does take a long time to make a bid you should not let this affect your decision. These are good habits to get into.

Even in the friendliest circles, where you get out your holiday snaps between hands and enjoy the evening as much for the gossip as the bridge, it can be annoying if your opponents continually take advantage of each other's mannerisms.

Lesson 155
More practice hands 1

Both vulnerable. Dealer South.

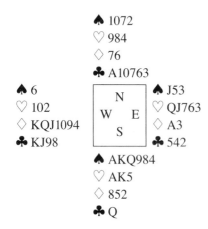

```
                    ♠ 1072
                    ♡ 984
                    ◇ 76
                    ♣ A10763
  ♠ 6                              ♠ J53
  ♡ 102          N                 ♡ QJ763
  ◇ KQJ1094   W     E              ◇ A3
  ♣ KJ98          S                ♣ 542
                    ♠ AKQ984
                    ♡ AK5
                    ◇ 852
                    ♣ Q
```

South	West	North	East
2♠	3◇	Pass	Pass
3♠	Pass	4♠	All Pass

Contract: Four Spades by South
Lead: king of diamonds overtaken by the ace, and after a diamond return to West's ten, West continues diamonds

First of all, let's look at the bidding. South is just worth an Acol Two bid but it is a marginal decision – if spades don't break he does not have his minimum eight tricks. Over the Three Diamond intervention, Three Spades and Four Spades retain their normal meaning. Without the overcall North would have bid a negative Two No-Trumps and then raised Three Spades to Four. With the overcall North must start with a pass (which is forcing – if West had not bid North-South could not have stopped below Three Spades, so there is no need for them to do so now) and then bid Four Spades.

At the table declarer hoped that West held the jack of spades. He ruffed the queen of diamonds with the ten of spades. However, East overruffed with the jack and returned a trump. Declarer ran off all his trumps but East made no mistake and in the end declarer had to lose a heart. Do you see how declarer could have done better?

He certainly needed a ruff in the dummy for his tenth trick. His trouble was that he tried to ruff the wrong suit. What he should have done was discard one of dummy's hearts on the third round of diamonds. Now there is nothing the defence can do. Declarer can win the next trick, draw two rounds of trumps and then cash the ace and king of hearts and ruff a heart with dummy's ten of spades. He then returns to hand with a club ruff and draws East's last trump.

Lesson 156
More practice hands 2

The last couple of hands in the book are designed to give you a taste of a frequently occurring advanced technique. Deal out the hands and make sure you can follow the play.

East-West vulnerable. Dealer South.

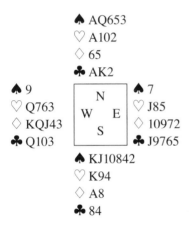

```
              ♠ AQ653
              ♡ A102
              ◇ 65
              ♣ AK2
   ♠ 9                      ♠ 7
   ♡ Q763        N          ♡ J85
   ◇ KQJ43    W   E         ◇ 10972
   ♣ Q103        S          ♣ J9765
              ♠ KJ10842
              ♡ K94
              ◇ A8
              ♣ 84
```

South	West	North	East
1♠	Pass	3♣	Pass
3♠	Pass	4♡	Pass
5◇	Pass	6♠	All Pass

Contract: Six Spades by South
Lead: king of diamonds

When South opened One Spade he gave North a bidding problem. His hand was much too good for a direct Four Spades but he did not have another suit. He settled for a jump shift of Three Clubs. If his partner raised him

he could always go back to spades. When South rebid Three Spades, North felt he was too good to sign off in game.

We said earlier that a jump shift was made on either a very good suit, a strong balanced hand, or a hand with a fit for opener. North's Four Heart bid showed that last hand-type. He has a club suit (well, nearly), a good spade fit and a control in hearts. Although South is minimum he is not ashamed of his hand and ought to own up to the ace of diamonds. That was enough for North to proceed to slam. Has North's bidding been too ambitious or do you see how South can succeed?

It looks as if declarer must lose a trick in each red suit. However, suppose he plays like this. He wins the ace of diamonds, draws trumps, cashes the ace and king of clubs and ruffs a club in his hand. Now he plays a diamond. Declarer and dummy have their original heart holdings along with lots of trumps. Suppose West wins the diamond. If he plays a minor suit, declarer will discard a heart from one hand and ruff in the other, enabling him to make the slam. So West plays a heart. Declarer plays low from dummy and East puts in the jack to force declarer's ace. Now declarer plays a low heart from hand, finesses the ten, and cashes the ace.

Because declarer has forced the opponents to open up the heart suit for him, one of his 'sure' losers has magically disappeared.

Lesson 157
More practice hands 3

A beginners' book is not really the place for advanced plays, but we thought it might be interesting for you to see a simple squeeze in operation.

No-one vulnerable. Dealer West.

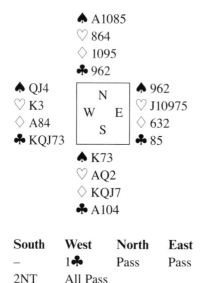

♠ A1085
♡ 864
◇ 1095
♣ 962

♠ QJ4   ♠ 962
♡ K3   ♡ J10975
◇ A84   ◇ 632
♣ KQJ73   ♣ 85

♠ K73
♡ AQ2
◇ KQJ7
♣ A104

South	West	North	East
–	1♣	Pass	Pass
2NT	All Pass		

Contract: Two No-Trumps by South
Lead: king of clubs

When West's One Club opening was passed round to him, South bid Two No-Trumps, showing 19–21 HCP. North passed, knowing that his side was unlikely to have 25 HCP.

When West led the king of clubs, South ducked a couple of rounds (simply as matter of general good technique) and won the third. He then played the king of diamonds from hand. West won his ace and cashed two more rounds of clubs. Declarer discarded a heart and a spade from both his own hand and from dummy. West then got off play with a diamond and South cashed his winners in that suit. These were the remaining cards just before South cashed his last diamond:

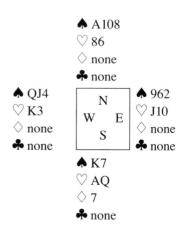

♠ A108
♡ 86
◇ none
♣ none

♠ QJ4   ♠ 962
♡ K3   ♡ J10
◇ none   ◇ none
♣ none   ♣ none

♠ K7
♡ AQ
◇ 7
♣ none

On the last diamond, what does West discard? If he throws a spade dummy's ten will make the last trick; if he throws a heart declarer will cash the ace dropping his king (the odds are in favour of West holding the king of hearts because of East's pass of One Club – West looks as if he has a balanced hand, so must have at least 15 HCP since he didn't open a 12–14 One No-Trump).

Lesson 158
Test your understanding 1

Finally, three hands to test your understanding of some of the more difficult aspects of this beginners' course.

South	West	North	East
1NT	Pass	2♣	Pass
2♠	Pass	4♠	All Pass

West leads the three of clubs. Plan the defence.

1 You are South with both sides vulnerable. You hold:

♠ Q2
♡ A643
◇ A5
♣ Q10652

What do you bid after the following sequences:

(A)
South	West	North	East
–	–	1NT	Pass
?			

(B)
South	West	North	East
–	1♡	2♠	Pass
?			

2

♠ Q865
♡ AK85
◇ 5
♣ KJ108

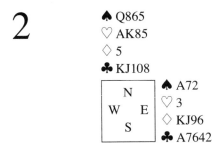

♠ A72
♡ 3
◇ KJ96
♣ A7642

3

♠ 763
♡ Q4
◇ 82
♣ AKJ964

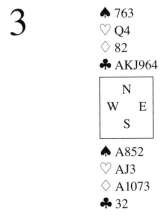

♠ A852
♡ AJ3
◇ A1073
♣ 32

South	West	North	East
1NT	Pass	3NT	All Pass

West leads the six of hearts which goes to East's ten and your jack. It looks as if you need to bring in the club suit so at trick two you play a club and, much to your delight, West plays the queen. Over to you.

Solutions
Test your understanding 1

1 On Sequence (A) you should bid Two Clubs, Stayman. If partner has four hearts, you bid Four Hearts, otherwise settle for Three No-Trumps.

On Sequence (B) you should bid Four Spades. Your partner has shown a sound opening bid with a good six-card spade suit. You have 12 HCP with two aces, an honour in partner's suit, a potential ruffing value and a possible source of tricks in clubs – that should be plenty for game. You do not need to look any further for a trump suit when you have a doubleton and know your partner has a six-card major.

2

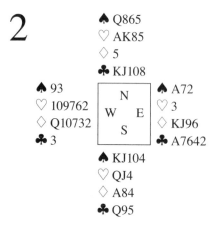

♠ Q865
♡ AK85
◇ 5
♣ KJ108

♠ 93
♡ 109762
◇ Q10732
♣ 3

♠ A72
♡ 3
◇ KJ96
♣ A7642

♠ KJ104
♡ QJ4
◇ A84
♣ Q95

It looks certain that your partner has led a singleton. You could give him a ruff immediately but you need four defensive tricks, not just three. The answer is to take your ace of clubs and switch to your singleton heart. When declarer plays a trump, you hop up with your ace, play the *seven* of clubs (suit-preference signal) to give partner a ruff, after which he will give you a heart ruff for the fourth defensive trick.

3

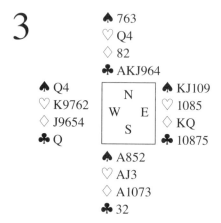

♠ 763
♡ Q4
◇ 82
♣ AKJ964

♠ Q4
♡ K9762
◇ J9654
♣ Q

♠ KJ109
♡ 1085
◇ KQ
♣ 10875

♠ A852
♡ AJ3
◇ A1073
♣ 32

Count your tricks. You have four tricks outside the club suit so need only five club tricks. Duck the queen of clubs and guarantee five club tricks. If you win the first club and the queen was a singleton, you will make only three club tricks and go down in your laydown game.

Lesson 159
Test your understanding 2

1 You are South with neither side vulnerable. You hold:

♠ AKJ10763
♡ 2
◇ 653
♣ 53

What do you bid after the following sequences:

(A)
South	West	North	East
–	–	–	1♡
?			

(B)
South	West	North	East
–	–	1NT	Pass
?			

2

♠ 93
♡ 762
◇ AQJ862
♣ 84

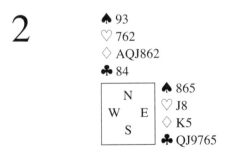

♠ 865
♡ J8
◇ K5
♣ QJ9765

South	West	North	East
2NT	Pass	3NT	All Pass

West leads the queen of spades which declarer wins with the king. He now plays the ten of diamonds from his hand. Your partner plays the four and dummy the two. Over to you.

3

♠ A43
♡ 43
◇ A62
♣ A7652

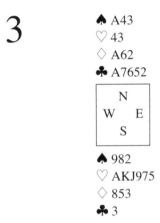

♠ 982
♡ AKJ975
◇ 853
♣ 3

South	West	North	East
–	1♣	Pass	Pass
1♡	Pass	1NT	Pass
2♡	Pass	3♡	All Pass

West leads the king of clubs against your Three Hearts. You win the ace as East plays the ten. Plan the play.

Solutions
Test your understanding 2

1 On Sequence (A), you should overcall Three Spades. Double jump overcalls at the three or four level show more or less the same as opening bids at those levels, i.e. long strong suits with little outside.

On Sequence (B), you should take a pot at Four Spades. There is no way of finding out whether partner's hand fits well with yours so there is no point in trying to bid scientifically.

2

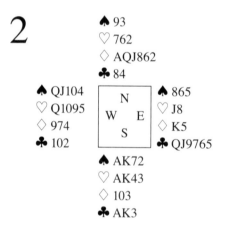

♠ 93
♡ 762
◇ AQJ862
♣ 84

♠ QJ104
♡ Q1095
◇ 974
♣ 102

♠ 865
♡ J8
◇ K5
♣ QJ9765

♠ AK72
♡ AK43
◇ 103
♣ AK3

Your best hope is that declarer has only a doubleton diamond, in which case, you must duck the first round of the suit. *You* know that declarer can now drop your king, but, provided you play smoothly, *declarer* does not. He will have no reason to do other than finesse again, in which case he will make only one diamond trick and as he has only six other tricks you will beat the game.

3

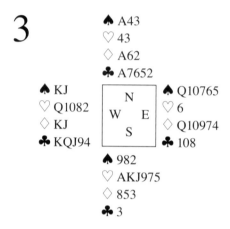

♠ A43
♡ 43
◇ A62
♣ A7652

♠ KJ
♡ Q1082
◇ KJ
♣ KQJ94

♠ Q10765
♡ 6
◇ Q10974
♣ 108

♠ 982
♡ AKJ975
◇ 853
♣ 3

You could take a heart finesse, hoping to make six trump tricks to go with three outside winners, but there is a better play. At trick two ruff a club, cross to an ace and ruff another club, then cross to the other ace and ruff a third club. Now you just need three tricks from your AKJ of trumps. Play a loser and hope West has to win. Unless East gets the lead, you cannot go down; if East does get the lead, discard until all you have left are trumps (if he plays a trump, win and play another loser). The worst scenario is that East is on lead at trick eleven when all you have left are trumps; if that is the case, your contract will depend on the heart finesse (though you may know that East cannot have the queen for his pass over One Club). By postponing the key play you lose nothing and may gain a lot. On the actual lay-out, the defenders must be card-perfect to beat you (can you work out how?).

Lesson 160
Test your understanding 3

1 You are South with East/West only vulnerable. You hold:

♠ QJ1065
♡ A7
◇ 9842
♣ 72

What do you bid after the following sequences:

(A)
South	West	North	East
–	–	1♠	Pass
?			

(B)
South	West	North	East
–	1♡	1♠	2♣
?			

2

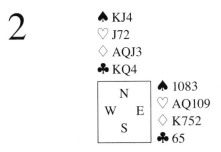

♠ KJ4
♡ J72
◇ AQJ3
♣ KQ4

♠ 1083
♡ AQ109
◇ K752
♣ 65

South	West	North	East
–	Pass	1◇	Pass
1NT	Pass	2NT	Pass
3NT	All Pass		

West leads the two of spades against Three No-Trumps. Declarer plays low from dummy and wins your ten with his queen. He next plays the ten of diamonds from his hand, which you allow to hold and another diamond to dummy's jack and you win with the king (your partner playing high-low). How do you hope to beat Three No-Trumps.

3

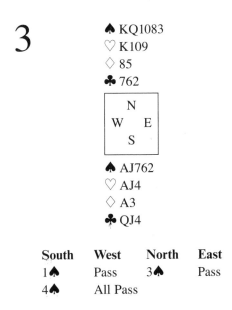

♠ KQ1083
♡ K109
◇ 85
♣ 762

♠ AJ762
♡ AJ4
◇ A3
♣ QJ4

South	West	North	East
1♠	Pass	3♠	Pass
4♠	All Pass		

Against your Four Spades West leads the ace of clubs followed by the king of clubs and another club, East following with the eight, nine and ten. Which defender will you play to hold the queen of hearts?

Solutions
Test your understanding 3

1 On Sequence (A) you should bid Three Spades. Your fifth spade is a reason to upgrade the hand but there is no need to go mad – partner will go on to game unless he is minimum.

On Sequence (B) you should bid Four Spades. You must hope that either your partner will make Four Spades or that it will be a good sacrifice. When you know that you have a ten-card fit and both the opponents are bidding it is time to be aggressive and make life difficult for them.

two spades, one heart, three diamonds and three clubs. However, maybe you can take five tricks first. Your only hope is in hearts. The trouble is that if you switch to the ten of hearts, declarer will run it round to his jack, giving him a second stopper in the suit. What you must do is switch to the *queen* of hearts. Now when your partner gets on lead with the ace of spades he can play another heart through dummy's jack and you will take three tricks in the suit to go with the two you already have.

2

♠ KJ4
♡ J72
◇ AQJ3
♣ KQ4

♠ A762   ♠ 1083
♡ 863   ♡ AQ109
◇ 86   ◇ K752
♣ J1097   ♣ 65

```
        N
    W       E
        S
```

♠ Q95
♡ K54
◇ 1094
♣ A832

You know your partner started with Axx2 in spades (without an honour he would have led his second highest). There is no room for him to have either the ace of clubs or king of hearts (or South would not have enough for his raise to Three No-Trumps). So, you know that declarer can develop nine tricks:

3

♠ KQ1083
♡ K109
◇ 85
♣ 762

♠ 94   ♠ 5
♡ Q87   ♡ 6532
◇ J1074   ◇ KQ962
♣ AK53   ♣ 1098

```
        N
    W       E
        S
```

♠ AJ762
♡ AJ4
◇ A3
♣ QJ4

You should make your game whoever has the queen of hearts. Just win the queen of clubs, draw trumps and play ace and another diamond. Whichever defender wins that trick will have to lead a heart or give you a ruff and a discard, either of which will give you your contract.

Glossary

attitude signal – the play of a high/low card to show you like/dislike the *suit* led

auction – the *bidding* stage of each deal

balanced hand – one with no *singleton* or *void* and no more than one *doubleton*

bid – a contract for a certain number of *tricks* in a particular *denomination*

bidding – part or all of an *auction*

block/blockage – inability to take all the winners in a suit because of high cards in the hand with the fewer cards

break – the distribution of the cards in a suit between the two hands of the partnership

call – a *pass*, *bid*, *double* or *redouble*

contract – the last bid in the *auction*

control – an ace or king, *singleton* or *void*

convention/conventional bid – a 'coded' *bid* showing a hand unrelated to the *suit* bid

count signal – the play of a high/low card to show an even/odd number of cards in the *suit* led

cross-ruffing – alternately ruffing in first one hand and then the other

cue-bid – either (a) a bid to show a *control* rather than length in a suit, or (b) a bid of an opponent's suit to show a strong hand

deal – (a) one complete hand of bridge, including the *bidding* and the *play*, (b) to distribute the 52 cards between the four players

deck – pack of cards

declarer – the first person to bid the *denomination* set as trumps in the *auction*

declaring side – *declarer*'s partnership

defender – one of the *declarer*'s opponents

defending side – the *declaring side*'s opponents

denomination – one of the four *suits* or *no-trumps*

discard – fail to follow suit (but not with a trump)

divide/division – see *break*

double – a *call* in the *auction* which doubles the stakes

doubleton – just two cards in a suit

duck – fail to win a *trick* that could have been won

dummy – *declarer*'s partner (or his *hand* which is laid face up on the table after the opening lead)

entry – a high card allowing access to winners

finesse – the attempt to win tricks with lower-ranking cards by taking advantage of the favourable position of the opponents' higher-ranking cards

fit – the number of cards in a suit held by one side

following suit – playing a card in the same suit as the one led

forcing bid – a bid you must not pass

give preference – show which of partner's suits you prefer

hand – the thirteen cards dealt to one player

high-card points (HCP) – 4 for an ace, 3 for a king, 2 for a queen and 1 for a jack

honour cards – ace, king, queen, jack (and sometimes ten)

honour sequence – three or more consecutive *honour cards*

invitational bid – a bid partner should only pass with a minimum hand

jump bid – a *bid* made at a level higher than necessary

jump overcall – an *overcall* made at a level higher than necessary

jump shift – an immediate response in a new suit at a higher level than was necessary

LHO – left-hand opponent

limit bid – a bid that describes a hand within narrow limits

major suits – spades and hearts

minor suits – diamonds and clubs

natural – showing the suit named

non-vulnerable – not yet having made a game (penalties cost less than when *vulnerable*)

no-trumps – the highest-ranking *denomination* which refers to play without *trumps*

open the bidding – start the *auction*

opening lead – the first card played to the first *trick*

overcall – a *bid* made after the opposition have opened

pack – all 52 cards

partner – the player sitting opposite

pass – signification of no wish to bid in the *auction* for the time being

play – the trick-taking part of each deal

pre-emptive bid – a *jump bid* made to make life difficult for the opponents

protective bid – a bid made after another bid has been followed by two passes

quantitative – natural and invitational

rank – either *majors* or *minors*

rebid – a second bid made by the same player

redouble – a call made after a *double* which redoubles the stakes

responder – the partner of the opening bidder

response – a bid made by the partner of the opening bidder

reverse – a bid, at the level of two or more, which shows a strong hand, that is made in a higher-ranking suit than the one first bid

revoke – a failure to follow suit when you could have done so

RHO – right-hand opponent

ruff – the play of a *trump* when you have no cards in the suit led

singleton – only one card in a suit

slam – a *contract* of twelve or thirteen tricks

suit – spades, hearts, diamonds or clubs

suit-preference – a play of a high/low card in certain situations to show a liking for a higher-/lower-ranking suit

take-out double – a conventional double that asks partner to choose a suit

top tricks – the tricks that can be taken in top cards without losing the lead

trick – four cards, one played by each player

trump – the suit named in the final *contract*

unbalanced hand – a hand containing a *void*, a *singleton* or two or more *doubletons*

void – no cards in a suit

vulnerable – having already scored a game (penalties cost more)